Natural History of
Blackwater Falls
State Park

West Virginia Adventure Guide:
The Natural History of Blackwater Falls State Park

By
Emily Grafton

copyright ©2002 Emily Grafton
Second Printing 2007

To order additional copies of this book or for book publishing information, or to contact the author:

Headline Books, Inc.
P.O. Box 52
Terra Alta, WV 26764

Tel/Fax: 800-570-5951
Email: blackwater@headlinebooks.com
Web Site: www.headlinebooks.com

ISBN 0929915283

Library of Congress Control Number: 2001094507

PRINTED IN CANADA

DEDICATION

This book is dedicated to one of West Virginia's most dedicated plant taxonomists, Bill Grafton, for contributing his encouragement and great knowledge of West Virginia's flora to the completion of this book.

Forward

It was a small group that gathered for a bird walk early one August morning. After adjusting our binoculars, we set out to enjoy the typical late summer fare. We made our way along the lake shore and before long, goldfinches, barn swallows, killdeer, crows, ravens and a host of cedar waxwings had presented themselves to us.

As we turned to go back to the Nature Center, we heard the distinct sound of Canada geese intent on making a soft landing on Pendleton Lake. We waited for their arrival. Their approach put them in the water right before our eyes. It was a sight to remember, for as the flock descended, some of the birds were doing barrel rolls in anticipation of entering the water. I was awed by such a simple observation of what had become a common sight— Canada geese setting down on the lake—yet, I had never noticed the acrobatics.

Blackwater Falls State Park has become a special place to me. Over the past 17 years, I have come to realize that it is not just the incredible natural resources and stunning scenery that makes it so special. It is those things combined with the people who visit here. In my capacity as the park naturalist, my shared experiences have been many and varied.

Many visitors come to Blackwater not knowing what to expect—I think this is good, it makes every nature walk memorable. You never know what adventure is waiting ahead on the trail. Emily Grafton's descriptive narratives will enlighten and delight both the hiker and the reader.

Pat Hissom
Naturalist
Blackwater Falls State Park

Acknowledgments

I wish to express my deep gratitude to Frances Tekavec and to Jim and Mary Cassel for inviting me into their homes and sharing their special insights on the community of Davis and the history of the region.

I wish to express my love and appreciation to my friend Bonnie Shough for her continued moral support and editorial review. Also, special thanks to Dr. Ken Carvell for his review of the manuscript. In addition, warm thanks to Mike Caplinger, Pat Hissom and Helen Williams for their ideas and text review.

Permissions

Permission granted from West Virginia University Department of Biology for illustrations from Strausbaugh and Core's Flora of West Virginia.

Permission granted from The West Virginia University Extension Service for illustrations by Diane Stirrat used from *Common Birds of West Virginia.*

Contents

INTRODUCTION

"Every scrap of biological diversity is priceless, to be learned and cherished, and never to be surrendered without a struggle." *–E.O Wilson*

Nestled against the base of Canaan Mountain, Blackwater Falls State Park snakes along the rim of Blackwater River canyon. The region surrounding the park is characterized by a series of mountains, plateaus and deep ravines carved by fast-flowing, boulder-littered streams. It is a corrugated landscape hewn from the perpetual geological forces simultaneously lifting it higher from below while gnawing it down from above.

Within the park's boundaries, Blackwater River plunges over a 57-foot cataract falls to a frenetic westerly course. Just below the falls, the rapidly flowing water has gouged a 500-foot deep, quarter-mile wide canyon. Further downstream, the canyon depths reach nearly 1500 feet. From the mouth of the canyon, the river wildly tumbles on, mingling with other streams that feed the Mississippi River.

The story of the people and events from the past three hundred years of the region remain with us through a variety of existing landmarks.

The landscape presents a patchwork quilt stitched from the remnants of past destructive timbering and industrial activities. Historical documents present an unfavorable picture of industrial development of the area. Unraveled pieces of an ancient ecosystem striving to resurrect itself dominates the quilt, adding a mosaic of exquisite colors and textures.

Observe the lichen dappled rocks and dwarfed trees reaching skyward from every point on the horizon. Nature has been slowly recovering for the past eighty years from a man-made devastation so complete that only time alone

Drawing by David Hunter Strother from The Blackwater Chronicle *by John Pendleton Kennedy, 1853 New York*

can heal it. Where tranquil hiking trails now meander through quiet evergreen forests, smoke-belching trains once creaked and groaned under massive loads of felled trees. Pollution from pulp factories, as well as leather tanneries, literally killed the streams, while lumberjack saws rasped incessantly until the forests were denuded.

Despite the environmental disaster that decimated the landscape at the turn of the century, Blackwater Falls State Park now serves as a sanctuary for stressed out moderns seeking renewal by reconnecting with nature. Sheltered in the dark recesses of boulders, new plant and animal life continually emerges. Life is irrepressible! That a force greater than human beings maintains the biosphere quietly murmurs with every breeze whisking across the bogs. One can feel that energy simply by being there.

The 1,688 acres of the Park provides great opportunities for recreation coupled with an unobstructed view of nature. Winter provides an exhilarating backdrop of sparkling snow for hiking, skiing, snow shoeing and tobogganing. Spring, summer and fall allows access to magnificent vistas overlooking the canyon and waterfalls. Separate trails traverse through the forest for nature study, bird-watching, hiking, horseback riding and biking. A swimming pool and tennis courts are open for the summer months. A comfortable lodge provides meals and in-door recreation year round. Well maintained rooms and separate cabins are available with camping facilities available seasonally.

As we continue to carve up and rearrange the face of our planet, areas such as Blackwater Falls State Park have become priceless. The universe may be expanding but planet earth is not. So, we must carefully weigh every decision regarding our resources. Tiny soil organisms, trees, animals, the cycling of nutrients and water provide the life-support system from which we derive suste-nance. The history of this magnificent park may help us to understand how each ounce of wa-ter, animal, bug, moss, tree and fun-gus makes living a possibility for people as well.

Drawing by David Hunter Strother from The Blackwater Chronicle *by John Pendleton Kennedy, 1853 New York*

HUMANKIND AND NATURE

"....I am glad I shall never be young without wild country to be young in. Of what avail are forty freedoms without a blind spot on the map."
— Aldo Leopold

The global migration of human beings punctuated by unexpected twists of fate, permanently changed the nature of this knobby mountain plateau. A path through history as circuitous as the old Indian trails snaking across the Allegheny Highlands carried the people and the forces that vastly altered the environment of the Blackwater River basin. Ancient cultures left obscure footprints along the Blackwater. Native American grave sites furnish artifacts from rock shelters and a mound along the Cheat River.

We have few stories echoing the laughter of their children or their daily activity because Native American settlements were long gone from the area. Historians agree that Indians never heavily populated the rugged terrain of West Virginia. The trails they followed were mostly used for hunting expeditions to and from surrounding states. Even so, although early settlers did not find Indian villages in this area when they first arrived, they did have to contend with parties of Indians on hunting forays who considered this area their own hunting grounds and who fought fiercely against the encroachment of white settlers.

Lengthy volumes record the past 250 years of Tucker County history where Blackwater Falls State Park is located; however, the majority of known events occurred only with the last 120 years. The first settlers arrived in 1800. They lived lives of incredible hardship in what was then an impenetrable wilderness with severe winters of deep snows.

The history of the Blackwater region is tied to the whims of English kings, to an error in calculation by surveyors, and, most eventfully,

Drawing by David Hunter Strother from The Blackwater Chronicle *by John Pendleton Kennedy, 1853 New York*

"Getting Under Way" by David Hunter Strother from The Blackwater Chronicle *by John Pendleton Kennedy, 1853 New York*

to the entrepreneurs of the industrial revolution, followed by a subsequent wave of intrepid settlers.

LAND GRANTS AND FEARLESS "BUSHWHACKERS"

We need to take a giant leap backwards in history to obtain a perspective on how the political boundaries of the Blackwater River area developed. During early English colonialism, vast tracts of Eastern United States lands were deeded as favors to noblemen from reigning monarchs. The entire state of Maryland, granted to Lord Baltimore in 1632 as a giant political plum from King Charles I of England, borders the Blackwater Country (land in the Blackwater River Drainage area).

King Charles had many challenges and made many poor decisions, especially in his reluctance to share his wealth and power with Parliament. He soon lost his crown—and his head through the political maneuverings of Oliver Cromwell. Eventually, Parliament removed the Cromwell contingent and in 1660, brought young Charles II from exile in France. In order to reward his allies, Charles II capriciously granted Lord Hopton, the Culpepper family, and others, title to six million acres of American soil.

These six million acres lay within the as yet uncharted western portion of what was then Virginia territory right up to the southeastern border of Maryland and included those areas drained by the Blackwater River. The deed stated, somewhat nebulously, that the tract included all of the land between the "head fountain" (headwaters) of the Potomac River to the "head fountain" (headwaters) of the Rappahannock River. All land north of the Potomac River had been granted earlier to Lord Baltimore, and was fairly well explored.

For nearly a century and a half, only a few settlers ventured into western portions of the Northern Neck region. High up in the misty Allegheny Mountains of the Northern Neck, the Blackwater River continued to flow unknown to the civilized world just as it had for thousands of years.

Time flowed on also. In 1688, Lord Culpepper (one of the recipients of King Charles II's bounty) bought out the other owners and King James II (a successor to King Charles II) made the title transfer legal. This immense estate eventually passed on to his only child and sole heir, Lady Catherine Fairfax, wife of Lord Thomas Fairfax. This land then passed to Catherine's son, also known as Lord Thomas Fairfax. Throughout these succeeding generations of ownership, profits from tenants and crops returned to the owners in England.

However, by the time Thomas junior received ownership, land-hungry English colonists were expanding further into the wilderness and homesteading where they found land suitable for farming. Apparently, the colonial governing body of Virginia had dispensed land grants to people in the eastern sections of the Fairfax tract. As a result of this activity, Lord Fairfax moved to America in 1735 to oversee his estate and to challenge the Virginia Assembly. Upon being told by the governing representatives of the Virginia Colony that there were no clear boundaries marking his lands, Lord Fairfax insisted that the English government organize a survey party to determine and fix the boundaries of his rightful ownership. Up to this point in time, neither the "first fountain" of the Potomac nor the Rappahannock had been officially located.

An incredible journey was begun by a party of eight surveyors in November of 1736 to accurately locate the headwaters of the Rappahannock and Potomac Rivers. They divided into two groups, one to survey the Potomac and one to survey the Rappahannock. Why this group ventured into the wilderness with winter approaching remains a mystery. One example of the harsh circumstances of their journey is the story of the time they completely ran out of food and were drawing lots to see who would become dinner.

William Mayo, who made a rough map of the region as they progressed, led the team exploring the Potomac. The map includes the Indian names for rivers and other sites. Mayo recorded that Indian hunting parties moving through the area provided the explorers with information about existing landmarks.

According to his report, the men followed the main branch of the Potomac River and found the mouth of the South Branch. They traveled on to where they came to the mouth of the North Branch. Based on his information, they followed the North Branch believing it led to the primary source or "fountain head" of the Potomac. What they did not realize was that a rainstorm had flooded the North Branch causing it to appear to be the larger of the two streams. This error significantly increased Lord Fairfax's holdings.

As they ascended from the valley higher into the mountains, it led them to a section of the eastern continental divide. There, just below the crest on the eastern flank of what is now Backbone Mountain, a spring was marked as the "head spring" of the Potomac. The water flowing from this spring as well as all other streams on the eastern side of the mountain flow to the

Atlantic Ocean. Streams originating just over the crest on the western side of Backbone Mountain, including the Blackwater River, flow to rivers that eventually make their way to the Gulf of Mexico.

The South Branch is actually the larger stream and thus its headwaters are the true "head spring" of the Potomac. This forty-mile error gave much more land to Lord Fairfax of Virginia, at the expense of Maryland, including most of current eastern panhandle of West Virginia along with portions of what is now known as Tucker, Grant and Randolph Counties. Maryland did eventually dispute the boundaries between the two states but lost most of the court battles to reverse the situation.

Ten years after the first excursion, in 1746, a second survey party was organized to generate better-detailed maps of the exact boundary line between the "head fountain" of the Potomac and Rappahannock. Thomas Lewis, one of the forty men who undertook this journey, kept a daily journal, from which we have an excellent description of the location of the Fairfax Line and of the topography near Blackwater Falls. He described portions of the Allegheny Front, Cabin Mountain and Canaan Valley through which the Fairfax line was marked. This survey

THROUGH THE WOODS.

"Through The Woods" by David Hunter Strother,
Virginia Illustrated *by Porte Crayon, 1857 New York*

began at the head of the Rappahannock River
on September 10, 1746, which currently lies
within the boundaries of the Shenanadoah National Park in Virginia. They reached the head
spring of the Potomac on October 22, 1746. It
took them nearly 43 days to travel approximately
76 miles.

Lewis wrote:
*"Tuesday 14ᵗʰ one of the Pilots horses
being missing a great part of the morning
was spent in vain hunting for him. Began
where we let off the Day Before Thence 100
poles a Loral Swamp Begins 406 poles X the
River of Styx total for this Day This River was
called Styx from the dismal appearance of*

this place Being Sufficen to Strick terror in any human creature ye lorals Ivey & Spruce pine so Extremely thick in ye Swamp through which this River Runs that one Cannot have Lest prospect Except they look upwards the water of the River of Dark Brownish Cooler & its motion So Slow that it can hardly be said to move its depth about 4 feet the bottom muddy & Banks high, which made it Extremely Difficult for us to pass the most of the horses when they attempted to ascend the farthest bank tumbling with their loads back in the river. Most of our baggage that would have been damaged by water were *Brought over on mens Shoulder Such as Powder, Bread and Bedclothes &.."*

According to calculations recorded in Fanslers' **History of Tucker County**, the men were 68 miles into their journey at the "River of Styx," just eight and one-half miles from their destination. The name of the 'River Styx' that Lewis gives to the stream refers to the dark and dreaded river in Greek Mythology over which dead souls had to be ferried to the underworld. The place must have been desolate and dismal indeed. It is believed that Lewis description of the "River of Styx" is of a tributary of the Blackwater River in Canaan Valley, probably Glade Run. It was to take another eight days for them to make the remaining nine-miles through the spruce swamps and rhododendron thickets of Canaan Valley and up over Brown Mountain to their destination.

The first of five "Fairfax Stones" was placed at the springhead near a tree marked with an X by the first survey team ten years earlier. They marked a tree for every mile they traversed. Eighty-six trees in all were marked. Most of those original trees have been felled or died, but a few do remain. They actually overshot their destination by one mile, but corrected the line on the way back. When you consider that the only equipment they had at the time was a simple transect, their accomplishment was phenomenal.

Lord Fairfax remained in the colonies selling off tracts of his land to eager settlers. Unfortunately for him, he remained loyal to the crown until the English were defeated. His remaining holdings thus became property of the victorious colonial government. These lands were granted as payment to many Revolutionary War patriots.

It was nearly a half-century later before we have record of any further human activity in the Blackwater Country. Three brothers and their families by the name of Fansler (recorded as Fanschler in older texts) left the "crowded" Shenandoah Valley in search of open land to farm. A popular legend quoted in one text on West Virginia history was attributed to Henry Fansler. In April of 1800 his party stood on the summit of Cabin Mountain gazing into the twenty-mile long valley. Awestruck by the view, Fansler exclaimed, "Besiehe das Land Kanaan!" (Behold the land of Canaan). Thus, the name Canaan Valley was born.

He was so enamored by the area that he informed his wife and children that they had just found their new home. His more dubious brothers took their families on to the more level lands of Ohio. That summer, the Henry Fansler family constructed a rough, one-room cabin and cleared enough land for crops and livestock. According to some accounts, they lasted three years. What Henry Fansler did not know, and perhaps his brothers suspected, was that this land had the harshest climate in all of West Virginia, mostly due to the elevation. Subsequent generations of Fansler's relate how the snows became nine feet deep that first winter and the temperature stayed well below zero for weeks. The family nearly froze to death and starvation was a constant threat. The next two winters were not much better and the summer crops did poorly in the short growing season. Henry had to constantly forage alone in a hostile environment for food for his family imprisoned in a tiny cabin encircled by a frozen world. During these three years, Mrs. Fansler gave birth to two babies. One wonders how she kept them warm and dry enough to survive in a miserable wooden cabin with little heat while she worried about their fate should Henry fail to return.

Near the end of their third year, Fansler sought out a more tolerable environment in which to live. During the summer of 1803, the Fansler family moved to the mouth of the Black-water River what only is now the town of Hendricks. The land and climate were so much more habitable that Henry named his new home Eden. The next Canaan Valley settler, Simon Cosner, did not arrive until 1864. He stayed, but even by the turn of the century, only a half-dozen or so families had settled there.

THE IRON HORSE OPENS A DOOR TO THE WILDERNESS

The one hundred and forty-one square mile area drained by the Blackwater River did not see any development until the end of the nineteenth century. The mountainous terrain draped with a dense, tangled forest of trees and rhododendron "dungeons" was too foreboding. In the meantime, a burgeoning civilization, well

"Passing The Laurels" by David Hunter Strother,
Virginia Illustrated *by Porte Crayon, 1857 New York*

entrenched along the east coast of the United
States, was on the verge of spilling westward
through Blackwater Country.

The completion of the Northwestern Road (now Rt. 50) in 1832, from Winchester, Virginia to Parkersburg on the Ohio River, allowed easy access to within twenty miles of the Blackwater River. Until the arrival of the railroad, twenty years later, this dirt road carried thousands of people into the interior of the country. The golden age of stagecoach travel and gracious inns, serving bountiful meals, had a glorious, but short life along the Northwestern Road. In these inns along the skinny thread of highway, tales of wilderness adventure shared around the fireplace at night fired imaginations. No one adventurer was to be outdone, and the stories often crossed the threshold between reality and fancy.

The completion of the Baltimore & Ohio Railroad to Oakland, Maryland in 1842, made western travel much easier. The northwestern Road actually fell into disrepair for the remainder of the nineteenth century. The invention of the automobile was to generate a demand for its revival early in the twentieth century.

From 1832 to 1842, completion of the B&O Railroad was

Illustration by David Hunter Strother from The Blackwater Chronicle *by John Pendleton Kennedy, 1853 New York* stalled at Cumberland, Maryland, while the Pennsylvania State Legislature debated whether to grant authorization to continue the line through their state in its course toward Wheeling on the banks of the Ohio River.

However, as luck would have it, the farmers of the rich farming region of Pennsylvania fought with a vengeance to keep the obnoxious smoke spewing trains from their lands. Actually, they feared the trains would put an end to the use of wagons and animals for hauling goods; and, their livlihood depended on the sale of their crops to feed hundreds of pack animals.

Finally, the Pennsylvania Legislature yielded to their constituents and said no to the railroad. Virginia happily stepped into the breach, and thus the B&O Railroad was completed over the extremely rugged terrain of what is now northern West Virginia. These events brought the railroad much closer than it would have been to the isolated landscape of the Blackwater River. This large island of unsettled land extended from the Blackwater area up over the Allegheny Front and across North Fork Mountain to the east.

What was to so successfully put this region "on the map," was the publication of *The Blackwater Chronicle*, in 1853. Copiously reprinted nationwide, and in several foreign languages, it was a dramatic, sometimes tediously chivalric account of the first of several fishing expeditions led by Phillip Pendleton Kennedy into the Blackwater River Canyon.

Based on the record of their first expedition, it is believed that the group reached the North Fork of the Blackwater River and camped beside the 30-foot high Douglas Falls. As Kennedy weaves his tale of adventure, he comments on the frolicking "good ole boy" one-upmanship of this all-male group, then sweeps into elaborate reflections on classic Greek mythology. A slight mental roller coaster for the modern reader, the following excerpt from Kennedy's narration illustrates the ambiance of the campsite.

> *"Our Blackwater villa is placed in the most picturesque position imaginable— almost immediately upon the banks of the most lovely of all amber streams. It is protected on one side by masses of gray sandstone rock, dashed with spots of a darker and lighter hue of gray, and occasionally a tinge of red—these rocks coated over in places with moss of various mingled colors—gray, blue, green, yellow and purple and soft and glossy as the richest velvet. A noble overshadowing fir tree rises up from one corner of the villa, some hundred and fifty feet, to the skies.*

THE MARCH.

"The March" by David Hunter Strother, Virginia
Illustrated *by Porte Crayon, 1857 New York*

> *The laurel grows thick and matted back of it,*
> *in impenetrable masses; and the glory of its*
> *flower, now just swelling into bloom, gives an*
> *air of elegance—even of splendor, to the*
> *embowered dwelling. In front, the pure cool*
> *stream leaps over the falls…and tumbles*
> *wildly down through its rocky and obstructed*
> *bed, filling your imagination with the poetry*
> *of unpolluted mountain waters—running*
> *pure to ideal, as the kingdom of heaven."*

What makes this book so intriguing to the
modern wilderness buff are the richly detailed
descriptions of the Blackwater region along with
the delightfully detailed drawings made by one
of his companions, David Hunter Strother. The
artist published his own stories in the widely read

Entering The Wilderness,
Harper's New Monthly
Magazine, *No. CCCLXII, July,*
1880, Vol. LXI

Harpers Monthly Bazaar beginning with the December 1853 issue. Both writers paint compelling pictures with their words.

To these adventure-loving men and to those who read their stories, it was a race against time to get to this mythical heavenly land before it was gone, and to see and experience what few men had dared. Even in the writings of these two sojourners, sadness is echoed that soon another magnificent forest reserve would be sacrificed to a resource-hungry nation. Kennedy uses the expression "unpolluted mountain waters" as though people were beginning to understand that unmanaged human activity could be destructive to the environment.

In 1857, George W. and William B. Dobbin purchased 26,000 acres of land, in the Cheat River watershed, from the Commonwealth of Virginia. This Baltimore family purchased a whole ecosystem, at a few dollars an acre, for a private wilderness retreat.

By 1859, the Dobbin family had only cleared 40 acres of their immense tract of land. They constructed a twelve-room log house just west of the falls of Pendleton Run, located within a mile of the current boundaries of Blackwater Falls State Park. In order to reach "Dobbin Manor," adventurous vacationers took the B&O from Baltimore to the last train stop at Oakland, Maryland. All food, tools, supplies and people had to be carted on packhorses across the remaining 25 miles through uninterrupted forest.

The "Dobbin House" became the summer home of the family and an endless parade of visitors. The guest list included a milieu of people representing wealthy Baltimore socialites, writers, painters, actors, and visitors from Europe. They came to hunt, fish, hike, make music, and "party." Their land also became known as "Blackwater Manor." Some called it "Canada" because of the Canadian-like climate and vegetation.

Some of the trails still criss-crossing the plateau and winding down to Blackwater Falls were made by the hundreds of visitors to Dobbin Manor as they made their way, carving their names into the rocks near the main falls of Blackwater River. Pearl Mott, author of *History of Davis* remembers seeing these carvings as a

Blackwater Falls, Harper's New Monthly Magazine, *No. CCCLXII, July, 1880, Vol. LXI*

little girl. Time and erosion have nearly erased the inscriptions.

The boundaries of Dobbin Manor extended to the south, down Blackwater Canyon to within a mile of Hendricks, then westerly to the crest of Backbone Mountain, and on to Canaan Mountain on the east. It remained a wilderness until sometime in the 1880's when the Dobbin family sold the timber and rented the lodge to the company of Henry Gassaway Davis. The lodge burned to the ground in 1888 while being used as a boarding house for the men building the West Virginia Central and Pittsburgh Railway.

The writing of Rebecca Harding Davis and

Dobbin House, Harper's New Monthly Magazine, *No. CCCLXII, July, 1880, Vol. LXI*

the drawings by one of her companions, artist Charles Graham, of their 1879 impromptu vacation to the Blackwater Country seem more reflective and equally poetic as Kennedy's. Rebecca published a story in the *Harpers New Monthly Magazine* in the June 1880 issue. The first few pages of this enjoyable article include a discourse on the challenges of finding an unspoiled location for a meaningful vacation. Her comments echo the sentiments of many people

Dobbin Fireplace, Harper's New Monthly Magazine, *No. CCCLXII, July, 1880, Vol. LXI*

today who seek to find solitude and untrammeled natural beauty at a reasonable price. Her following comments reflect modern sentiments.

"After him come pell-mell the would-be aesthetics, and later the mere fashionable, as the flock follows the tinkle of the bell-weather and up go the mammoth hotels as fast as mushrooms on a May morning."

Rebecca and her husband took the B&O Railroad out of Baltimore in search of scenery, and escape from the crowded "tourist traps." They had three weeks with no specific destination. On the train ride from Cumberland heading west, they met an old southern gentleman named Judge Hixley. He told them about the idyllic wilderness bordering the Blackwater River. "The wilderness," said the judge, "comprises seven hundred square miles of virgin forest, which will be a mine

Judge Hixley, Harper's New Monthly Magazine, *No. CCCLXII, July, 1880, Vol. LXI*

of wealth in timber some day, when it is opened up by a railway."

The fishing, hiking and camping in an incredibly remote and wild environment described by Judge Hixley was just the sort of venture Rebecca was seeking. So the party left the train at Oakland, Maryland, where they hired a driver, wagon and a team of oxen to take them to the edge of this near primeval forest where they would truly begin their quest—on horseback.

Just wide enough for a wagon, the road ended at Fort Pendleton Inn located near what is now Gormania, West Virginia. They then hired young Jerry Browning to lead them through twenty miles of trackless forest to the Blackwater River. Legends of the daring Meshach Browning, infamous bear hunter and father of Jerry, are still told by local residents of western Maryland and West Virginia.

The forest became oppressive and overwhelming in places as Rebecca's words

Jerry Browning, Harper's New Monthly Magazine, *No. CCCLXII, July, 1880, Vol. LXI*

Illustration by David Hunter Strother for The Blackwater Chronicle *by John Pendleton Kennedy, 1853 New York*

reveal in the succeeding passage from her story, *By Paths In the Mountains*.

"They rode Indian file along a trail which only Jerry's eyes could follow; it crossed heaps of rocks, swamps, fallen trees; it led through an unbroken forest of gigantic pines, oaks, birch, ash and sugar maples; even the nut trees and black cherry had time here to reach a height of one hundred and fifty feet. Evergreens and deciduous trees grew alike leafless and branch-less side-by-side, spreading palm-like at the top. The journey was in fact, a passage through interminable aisles of huge black pillars under a flat leafy roof. The sides of the creeks were banked with flaming color; laurel and rhododendrons heaped up walls of dark green, scarlet, and creamy white; in the sunshine late azaleas lifted wands of shell-like rose. Sometimes, the horses literally broke the path for miles through waving forests of fern.

"There was no sign that man had ever passed this way before. Huge trees, fallen a century before, lay in gigantic round furrows on the deep moss, of fretted and fluted lichen, gray and golden, bronze and purple, and of trailing myriads of pink oxalis. Plenty of fern nodded from the sides, a thicket of young hemlocks pushed ambitiously up from the top of the ridge; but when Jerry put his foot on it, the whole furrow crumbled like a puffball into a cloud of red dust. It was a dead body, which undisturbed in the slow passage of uncounted years had made all this false show of life. Very few songbirds had made their way into this solitude. The absolute stillness was strange and oppressive at noonday. Nature dwelt alone here, and kept silence, and there was something savage in her mood, now that they had come upon her unaware. Gloomy chasms open from either side; dense, dark laurel thickets choke every approach; hoary trees gather in conclave above and look down, shaking their heads with melancholy and foreboding; but through all the vigorous bright stream leaps and shouts with a mad joy. It is the very soul of youth in the region of Age and Death."

During their three-week stay, the party lived off the land. They feasted on venison, trout and, no doubt, other wild game. A few members of the group, including Charles Graham walked to the Dobbin House. They found the building in disrepair but occupied by a party of artists, sportsman and guides.

When Rebecca Harding Davis published her story, this handiwork of eons was less than a decade from obliteration.

The growing economic and industrial climate in the cities that created a middle class and the concept of "vacations" were the same forces that led to the intensive exploitation of its resources.

By-Paths, Harper's New Monthly Magazine, *No. CCCLXII, July, 1880, Vol. LXI*

HENRY GASSAWAY DAVIS: THE END OF THE WILDERNESS

"Like winds and sunsets, wild things were taken for granted until progress began to do away with them"—Aldo Leopold

As the hunting expeditions of the early 1850's commenced, the wheels of fate were turning in another direction in the heart and soul of a young entrepreneur named Henry Gassaway Davis.

Born into a successful Presbyterian Calvinist family with a tireless work ethic, Davis was conditioned early to become one of the east's most successful businessmen. However, his father lost all of the family's resources in the economic panic of 1837. Without so much as a whimper, his mother set about creating ways to earn money to support herself and her family.

After experiencing a life of luxury and association with the upper class members of society, Davis found himself working as a water boy at a rock quarry. He demonstrated tireless energy and enthusiasm for his job, ignoring the snubbing he received from previous companions.

The quarry closed and an old friend of the Davis family hired Henry to oversee the day-to-day operations of his plantation.

However, it was the power and excitement of the approaching B&O Railroad that drew Henry like a magnet, much as it did many young men at the time. He was hired as a brakeman. His intelligence, hard work and character attracted the notice of those higher up in the industry. And after only a year, he began to move quickly up the ranks.

Although I have alluded to the unique abilities of Henry Gassaway Davis, the majority of his phenomenal success was due to juxtaposition. The wealth of the forest and mineral resources still hidden in the Allegheny Highlands south of the B&O had not yet caught the eye of anyone with the money or the vision to develop them. But Henry noticed.

Fungous Growth In the Wilderness, Harper's New Monthly Magazine, *No. CCCLXII, July, 1880, Vol. LXI*

Immediately after his move to Piedmont, the indefatigable Davis helped his brothers establish a local coal and

Undisturbed woods on a trubutary of the Blackwater River, courtesy of the West Virginia Geology Survey

lumber business in Piedmont. They also jointly opened a large general store. In 1858, he left the railroad to form the Bank of Piedmont and to help manage his brothers' businesses. His success story from then on is a real head spinner.

The most lucrative segment of his business ventures relates to the Blackwater River drainage area and with the establishment of a railroad line from Piedmont into the land of the Blackwater River. The rise of the boomtown of Davis, and subsequent lumbering and mining activities he made possible, left an indelible mark on the communities and topography of this area.

While living in Piedmont, Henry had made several long forays into Canaan Valley and across the Allegheny Plateau to the present site of Blackwater Falls State Park. He realized that if he could establish a transportation system in and out of this wilderness, then he could control the development of the timber and minerals there.

Above; Kitzmillers, right;
Mountain Weaver,
Harper's New Monthly
Magazine, *No. CCCLXII,*
July, 1880, Vol. LXI

Above; Regiment, right; Omish Woman, below; Miller, Harper's New Monthly Magazine, *No. CCCLXII, July, 1880, Vol. LXI*

During the Civil War, the Davis brothers made a fortune supplying the B&O with timber and other supplies. They were Unionists and made their mark supporting the Union efforts to control the railroad. So, by the end of the war, Henry was in a financial position to expedite the plans he had envisioned for harvesting the huge coal reserves and, what has been considered to be the finest red spruce and northern hardwood forests in the world.

Davis managed to get himself elected to the West Virginia Legislature in order to generate the political power to get his empire underway. Serving on the Roads and Internal Navigation Committee, he, and several partners, acquired a charter to form the Potomac and Piedmont Coal and Railroad Company. This blatant co-mingling of business and politics dominated the era across the nation and the effects still affect us today. The decisions made and laws passed gave business interests a sort of carte blanche they had not previously had.

The first tracks of the railroad, a distance of 57.6 miles, were laid over a span of four years as the railroad ties were driven through the forest and muscled into the landscape between Piedmont and Davis.

Between 1880 and 1884, the railroad

company reorganized to become the West Virginia Central and Pittsburgh Railway. Davis and his brothers also purchased several other tracts of unbroken forestland in what was to become the Fairfax and Davis districts of Tucker County. They paid about $.57 an acre for 23,550 acres as revealed by a search of the county records by Henry Floyd Fansler. They purchased another 34,806 acres adjacent to the first tracts by the end of 1883. By the Spring of 1884, he had acquired nearly half a million acres of land to exploit for coal and timber.

He then hired Robert Eastham, a colorful character who had been farming in Canaan Valley since 1876, to clear a parcel of land in the midst of a vast tract of red spruce where Beaver Creek joins the main fork of the Blackwater River. Eastham set up a camp near Beaver Creek and secured local help for this immense task.

A civil engineer named James Parsons laid out the streets of the future town after the trees were cleared. He was hired to divide this area into neat rows of streets to await the railroad and the people.

Once the transportation system was in place, Davis was finally able to shift his energies into building the town of Thomas. This town, located two miles north of Davis, was to become the center of his mining empire; he left the timber industry to others. Though Henry Gassaway Davis made an incredible fortune from coal, the most significant impact on the Blackwater drainage area lay in the clutches of the timber men.

In 1890, the main line of the West Virginia and Central Pittsburgh Railway was extended from Thomas along the North Fork of the Blackwater River. The railroad traversed the North Fork into the main gorge of the Blackwater River to Hendricks and beyond to Elkins, to connect the expanding coal and timber interests. It is this grade that the current Blackwater Canyon Rail Trail follows. This railroad was eventually incorporated into the Western Maryland Railroad System.

Two lumber-dependent businesses were in full operation in Davis in 1866. The first was the Jacob L. Rumbarger company followed by the LaDew Tanning Company. The lumber company stayed in business until 1924 when there was no longer a tree big enough to cut left standing within reach of the company's 65 miles of railroad.

NATURE'S BOUNTY DEPLETED; THE TIMBER INDUSTRY

It all began in the fall of 1883, when Jacob Leathers (JL) Rumbarger of Indiana journeyed to Canaan Valley in search of marketable timber.

Once established, he spent the better part of a year purchasing timber in the valley, hiring loggers and arranging for teams of horses and other necessary equipment for a logging operation. In the fall of 1884 the railroad reached Davis and Rumbarger built the first big band-sawmill between what is now second and third streets just below the mouth of Beaver Creek. The persistent endeavors of J.L. Rumbarger ushered in the forty-year reign of the timber industry in Davis.

By the fall of 1885, Rumbarger had cut several stands of cherry and red spruce. The spruce was skidded to landings along the river to await the spring floods that would carry the logs onto Davis. The cherry was hauled out of the valley on large horse-drawn sleds to the mill. The mill was designed for sawing hardwood trees. The spruce would have to wait for another mill to be built.

However, Rumbarger was not to lead that

Softwood Band Saw Mill of Babcock Lumber & Boom Company at Davis, Tucker County. This mill cut over 400 million feet of spruce from 1890-1911. Courtesy of the West Virginia Geological Survey

Pulp Mill at Davis, Tucker County. Photo courtesy of the West Virginia Geological

industry. A Mr. Albert Thompson arrived in the area in 1887. He and his partners had designs to cut and sell spruce and other softwood timber. He also maneuvered a permit from the state to

49

dredge the channel of the Blackwater River to make it easier to drive logs in the spring. Despite his success and hard work, Rumbarger left Davis soon after the arrival of Thompson and took up timbering in another part of the state.

After the exit of his rival, Thompson had the mill re-furbished to saw soft woods. He formed the Blackwater Boom and Lumber Company that remained in business until 1907.

From 1888 to 1907 Blackwater Boom and Lumber built primary railroad lines along several tributaries of the Blackwater River, including the Little Blackwater River and up along the north side of the main branch of Blackwater River into Canaan Valley. During these years the Blackwater Boom and Lumber Company operated very successfully. The company constructed a permanent rail line on the south side of the Blackwater River from Davis up onto Canaan Mountain that extended along the eastern rim to the crest of the mountain.

The primary sawmill, engine house, loading docks and lumber producing operations were located on the long strip of land behind the buildings currently lining William Street. One of two dams built on the Blackwater River was located in this area to hold logs before they entered the sawmill.

Pulp Wood at Davis, Tucker County. Photo courtesy of the West Virginia Geological Survey

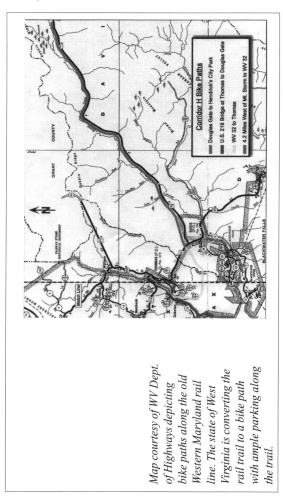

Map courtesy of WV Dept. of Highways depicting bike paths along the old Western Maryland rail line. The state of West Virginia is converting the rail trail to a bike path with ample parking along the trail.

Other businesses were located in Davis as a result of the timber boom, including a pulp mill started by the enterprising Luke brothers. They founded what was to become the dominant pulp and paper industry known today as Westvaco. In 1892, the Luke brothers formed the West Virginia Pulp Company when they purchased 50,000 acres of virgin spruce timber near Davis. They built a huge pulp-manufacturing factory by the river at the northern end of town in1895.

The Fayweather and Ladew Tanning Company established on the river at the south end of town was one of the largest in the country. This plant could process nearly seven hundred cowhides per day into leather. The cowhides were brought in on trains from large meat processing plants in Chicago. A primary resource needed by the tannery was the tannic-acid-rich bark of hemlock. Thousands of hemlock trees were cut, their bark removed for the tannery and the rest of the tree was often left to decay when the lumber market was flooded and the low-value hemlock wood could not be sold at a profit.

The cluster of houses on the hill across from the tannery was bombarded by pollution belching from the smokestacks of the tannery.

This section of town was dubbed "Vinegar Hill" because the smell was so bad. In 1919, the company closed its doors in response to labor strikes and demands for better working conditions and higher pay.

From 1886 until 1907, the Thompson brothers concentrated their timbering operations on the ridges and mountainsides easiest to reach from Davis. During this period, the company cut the timber along the crest of Canaan Mountain and down along the eastern flank to the valley. In 1895 the railroad on Canaan Mountain was extended another three miles to the headwaters of Red Run.

Beginning about 1900, the primary timber left in the region was on the western flank of Canaan Mountain down across the Blackwater Canyon and up toward Backbone Mountain, essentially most of the original 25,000-acre Dobbin Manor Tract. By 1902, the Thompson brothers had managed to purchase all of the timber rights to that tract.

During the years between 1900 and 1907, the first railroad lines were run into what is now Blackwater Falls State Park. The first line was built along the south canyon rim all the way to Lindy Run, near the famous Lindy Point overlook of Blackwater Canyon. Two side spurs were

Shay engines of Babcock Lumber & Boom Co., Davis, Tucker County 1912. Photo courtesy of West Virginia Department of Natural Resources.

built from this main line, a two-mile stretch up Engine Run and another two-mile line went up Shays Run. Both of these old railroad grades are now beautiful trails that wind through the park into the Monongahela National Forest.

The railroad was eventually continued from Lindy Run up over the crest of Canaan Mountain and into Red Run, near the area logged in the 1890's when the first line extended from Davis out across Canaan Mountain. By the time they were through building railroads, the logging railroads had made a complete circle around Canaan Mountain. The present day eighteen mile Canaan-Loop Road was created from this system of railroad grades.

In 1907, the Thompson Lumber Company was sold lock-stock and barrel to the Babcock Lumber and Boom Company. When the Babcock Company purchased the holdings, they had grown considerably. Included in the purchase were two sawmills, a box factory, forty miles of standard gauge railroad, 46,000 acres of remaining timberlands, a planing mill and eight and a half million feet of stacked lumber. The Babcock Company operated successfully until 1924.

The period of the Babcock family operation is probably one of the most colorful

Wreck of Shay No. 2148 near Davis, Turker County, 1918.
Photo courtesy of West virginia Department of Natural Resources

and flamboyant of the logging boom days in Davis and perhaps in the whole Eastern United States, even though the end of it brings to mind that dreadful scene in the Dr. Seuss film, *The Lorax.* When the last tree is cut, the music stops, the engines cease and everyone looks around dumbfounded at what has been done, and with slumped shoulders, and glum faces silently creep away. In the true-life scenario, many of the residents of Davis had nowhere else to go.

The Babcock's were lumbering magnates with timbering operations along the spine of the Appalachian Mountains from Pennsylvania to Georgia. They had a large capital base from which to improve the operations and contribute some new buildings to the community. They updated the mills, built a new one on the south side of the river below Davis, built a bank and huge Company store. Both of these buildings are still in use on the east end of town.

The new owners hired a talented and charismatic man named Fredrick Viering in 1908 to supervise the timber cutting in the woods. Under his supervision, the company built a railroad spur along the north rim of the canyon as far as Big Run; temporary stringer rails were run up along Big Run and Tub Run to the top of Backbone Mountain.

Camp On The Blackwater, Harper's New Monthly
Magazine, *No. CCCLXII, July, 1880, Vol. LXI*

After extracting all of the timber on the
north side of the canyon including the north wall,
the company began concentrating on the timber
on the rugged south wall of the canyon. A major
spur was run down into the canyon along the
south wall from Lindy Run, heading west
towards the mouth of the river. A third of the
way down, the track was reversed and
descended all the way to the bottom of the
canyon across from the mouth of the North Fork

of the Blackwater. Another spur headed further into the canyon to just below the present overlook at the lodge. All was completed around 1911.

The cut timber was hauled up out of the canyon by huge machines called skidders, stationary contraptions placed on a flatbed railroad car, housing a motor, a tall tower and a series of pulleys and cables. The cables could be extended in a wide arc up to 2500 feet away to drag logs from the steep canyon walls to the railroad tracks where they could then be hauled to the mills in Davis.

Representative from the Japanese and Russian governments came to observe the operations in order to gain knowledge that would help them successfully timber the rugged mountains of Taiwan and Siberia. Young college students studying forestry at what is now Michigan State University also came to observe all aspects of the lumber operation including the camps, skidders, railroads and mills.

William R. Morris, editor of the *Davis News* traveled with one of the Japanese teams of observers to the bottom of the canyon in 1914. He wrote a lengthy report for the paper describing his experience. The following quote is taken from his article.

"The afternoon was ideal for the trip, and to those who had never been over the line it was a rare treat. The fine view from the top of the gorge; the descent into the gorge; a drop of nearly a thousand feet; the zigzag railroad; ravines spanned by trestles; the sides of ridges cut away for the roadbed; shanties built in the air; the steaming, throbbing machinery lifting thousands of pounds of logs like so much cork and bringing them great distances and piling them at the feet of the loadermen; every man at his post and the entire operation going like clockwork."

Of course, things did not always go as planned. The work was rough and dangerous. There were occasional train wrecks; landslides, equipment failures and men were sometimes killed. Injuries slight and serious were a regular occurrence. However, for many of the men who worked in the operation, the challenge of the tasks overrode any thoughts about the risks.

Most of the timber had been removed from the canyon by 1916. It was a fantastic, incredibly well orchestrated engineering and technological event. Hundreds of men cut the trees, operated the skidders, maintained the railroad tracks and operated the trains and the mills. People came from all over the world to learn from this remarkable logging operation.

During the first few years of the operation in the canyon, the Babcock Company prepared special railroad cars for tourists who wished to descend the tracks into the canyon and observe the awesome timbering operations. It was exciting to ride along the narrow tracks into the deep canyon and marvel at the technology. But within a few years, the scene became desolate and hideously ugly, and the tourist season was over about as fast as it came. The final scene spoke loud and clear that something was wrong with our intensified technologies and system of resource extraction, a fact that no facet of society wanted to face.

After the canyon was logged, the Babcock operation began logging on the Allegheny Front near Dolly Sods. A railroad line had been run to the top of Cabin Mountain near Stony River from the northern end of Canaan Valley. The Babcock Company also timbered areas of Canaan Valley that had been logged twenty years prior to its establishment. Some virgin timber had been missed in a few places, and some new growth was big enough to cut.

The Babcock operations ceased in 1924.

Destruction of vegetation and soil by fires following lumber operations near Davis, Tucker County. Photo courtesy West Virginia Geological Survey.

The primary reason was the vanishing timber; however, a violent end to the life of their highly trusted and admired employee, Frederick Viering, accelerated the closing of the operations. The strong will and deep determination that fueled the accomplishments of Frederick Viering, were also to be his undoing.

Viering took one of the trains from Davis through Canaan Valley and over Cabin Mountain on February 5, 1924 to inspect the timbering operations. Ironically, the engine that pulled the train that day had been dubbed the *hoodoo engine* because it had been involved in several deadly wrecks. According to most historical accounts, Mr. Viering phoned his wife in Davis from the top of Cabin Mountain. He asked her to have his dinner ready for him, as he would arrive in one hour. The fireman working on the train told Viering that there was no way they were going to make it in an hour because the rails were iced over. The fireman is quoted with saying " you will go in a corpse if you try that." Viering is said to have replied, "I'll eat my supper with the old woman in Davis tonight, or I'll eat it with the devil in hell!"

As the train veered around a sharp curve near the bottom of the mountain, it picked up speed, went out of control and left the rails, crashing upside down in a bog. Mr. Viering lay crushed and scalded from the steam of the engines until a crew was able to reach the sight. The other men on the train either jumped clear before the train wrecked or were not badly injured. Viering probably died on impact, but whether he ate with the devil we shall hopefully, never know.

Whether or not people thought the timber would last forever or they simply chose not to think about forces beyond their control, the end must have been a devastating time in the lives of the merchants and blue-collar workers alike. There were many signs during the decade before 1924 of an impending economic and environmental apocalypse.

Blackwater Falls less than ten years after logging was terminated. Photo courtesy of West Virginia Geological Survey.

Above: Logging railroads in Blackwater Canyon, Tucker County, 1905. Photo courtesy West Virginia Department of Natural Resources.

Below: Close-up of Blackwater River Canyon less than ten years after logging. Photo courtesy of West Virginia Geological Survey.

When the timber had been completely removed from an area, particularly the spruce forests, the operation left drying piles of slash (tree tops and discarded limbs) and an unprotected soil. The soil dried out quickly from the exposure to sunlight and of course the slash dried as well. The land was a tinderbox waiting for a spark from any source. Fires fueled from engine sparks, careless smokers and even lightening were frequent occurrences across these areas. Often, the fires would smolder for weeks as they burned through the dried humus. Thousands of acres of once superb forests became wastelands of exposed boulders and bedrock.

Below, Henry Floyd Fansler describes the terrible fires in the Blackwater River Canyon as he experienced the environmental degradation while just a young boy. However, modern foresters question the accuracy of his memory in regard to the length of the fires at the location he describes. Fires would have burned quickly through the hardwoods in the canyons. It is possible that fires burned for weeks on the plateau where stands of spruce had been cut, and the deep humus left to dry. Quite possibly, he is referring to Davis and not Hendricks.

"When the fires occurred the peat burned and smoldered for months and only a heavy and protracted snow would extinguish it. Such a fire broke out in Blackwater Canyon, three miles above Hendricks, on May 30, 1914, and burned all summer. The sky over Hendricks was lighted with the reflection of the blaze to such an extent that one could sit on the platform of Harvey's store at midnight and read the afternoon paper……..Snows finally extinguished it on November 30, 1914, after burning six months to the day. All the rattlesnakes, copperheads and wild animals of the area hastened to get out with their young. This writer lay along the river bank, with his cousins, and shot them as they were swimming to safety….. a heedless, foolhardy destruction of wild game for which he is utterly ashamed, and for which he condemns himself along with the other despoilers of nature he now condemns……Two of the leading citizens of the state, Henry Gassaway Davis and his son-in-law Stephen Benton Elkin, both industrial giants and political powers, were proponents of a policy for the absolute destruction of the forests of Tucker County and adjoining counties.

*Their program was to cut every piece of
wood that would make a saw-log, mine-
prop, or pulpwood and deliberately burn
all that remained to convert it into a vast
grazing range. They threatened to break
the timber leases of lumber companies
that refused to go along with their
scorched earth policy."*

Fansler's passionate remorse of his
boyhood ignorance and of the greed of those
people who were leaders of the world into which
he was born, expresses feelings and lessons that
people seem unable to learn even today. The
industrial revolution unleashed in the last century,
was a runaway train that would not be stopped.
For no one on board, or within the vicinity of this
tumultuous series of events, tried to stop it.
Ignorance, greed and those with power stifled
the voices of the few who protested.

The few eyewitnesses mid-way in the
destruction, who publicly expressed their
concerns, include A. B. Brooks. He was a
prominent naturalist who expressed what was
happening in an issue of the *West Virginia
Geologic Survey* in 1911:

*"When the destruction was complete all
vegetable matter that wasn't soaked had*

burned, and with it all insects, worms, salamanders, mice and other burrowing forms of life. Bare rocks remained and thin mineral soil, this after several feet lower than ground level in the original forest."

Nearly a billion board feet of timber was cut and processed by the three companies which operated from Davis within a span of 40 years. This figure includes the following estimates reported in a *West Virginia Geological Survey Report*: 439,517,452 board feet of spruce, 272,450,227 board feet of hemlock and 450,180,040 board feet of hardwoods. And, much of the hemlock was cut only for its bark. Millions of board feet of hemlock wood was wasted.

The destruction from the rapacious clear cutting of the upland forests near Davis and throughout the Allegheny Mountains had equally great impacts further downstream. Chemical pollutants from the leather tanneries and pulp plants poisoned the Cheat River as far as Morgantown, West Virginia and Pittsburgh, Pennsylvania.

In response to the public outcry over the growing environmental problems, the governor of West Virginia formed the West Virginia

Natural Resource Commission in 1908. However, the industrial machine was a beast that would not be stopped too soon or too easily. The giants of industry had a grip on state and local governments. It would be a few more years when the devastation was complete, before much could be done.

Studies conducted by the *West Virginia Geological Survey* in 1911 revealed that the water in the Monongahela River (formed from the Cheat and West Fork Rivers) ruined the boilers of steamboats as a result of the corrosive action of the pollutants. It was reported that the water was so toxic that it would eat the hair off the legs of cattle wading in the water and kill those that drank it. A. B. Brooks reported that fish had been eliminated from the Cheat River from its headwaters to its mouth.

Deforestation from the timbering and the fires that followed had an even worse effect on the cities further downstream. Morgantown, Pittsburgh and Wheeling had terrible floods, particularly when the spring snows thawed. There was not enough vegetation to hold the water in the mountains. Even the soils were destroyed in places, leaving no place for the spring thaws and rains to go but the river channels.

The timber and coal barons and their out-of-state financial backers left with their fortunes and left the mess, a resource-depleted land and jobless communities to struggle on their own for a solution. The nation's and state's taxpayers would later pay the price. Ironically, those who believed that government should not hinder business in any way had no qualms about government paying to clean up the destruction they created.

An Old Inn on the way to Fort Pendelton, Harper's New Monthly Magazine, *No. CCCLXII, July, 1880, Vol. LXI*

Life In The Industrial Boom Days Of Davis

"One generation abandons the enterprises of another like stranded vessels."—Henry David Thoreau

The story of the town of Davis and nearby villages told only through the events of business ventures and industrial accomplishments is as hollow as the standing trunk of a dead tree. The decisions and power wielded by the few men who created the town and ran the show to suit their own needs, had an indelible impact on the lives of those who worked for them. Yet, the stories of the everyday folks of Davis are as full of courage, ingenuity and richness as those of the major players.

Much of what I can share with you about the good and bad, funny and sad days in Davis comes from those who lived through many years of the town's triumphs and turmoil. Much of the real history of Davis is not written anywhere; it lives primarily in the hearts and memories of the people who lived it. Pieces of history lie in scattered fragments along the railroad tracks from Davis to the damp, cool depths of idle coke ovens below Thomas, West Virginia.

Hewn from a virgin forest to a town of 25 houses within one year, Davis was dubbed "Stump town," as were many frontier towns throughout the United States. Robert Eastham had barely cut down the trees before people moved in. Stumps of those mighty giants were left in place and buildings constructed around them. People claimed they could walk from one end of Davis to the other from stump to stump, never touching the ground.

Davis was incorporated in 1889 with a population of 909 people, only five years after Robert Eastham had cleared the space. Those five years connected a ragged clearing in the forest to people from all over the western world. Many of the people who came to work and live in Davis and the nearby towns of Thomas, Coketon and Douglas were first generation European immigrants.

When the Babcock Company took over in 1907, most of the labor for the woods camps came by way of Ellis Island from Hungary, Slovenia, Germany, France, Italy, Sweden and Russia. The companies that needed laborers posted recruiters at Ellis Island. Most of the incoming immigrants did not speak a word of English. Unless a relative already working in the area had arranged for their travel to the area, they signed up with a recruiter at Ellis Island and would have absolutely no idea what fate had in store for them.

A woman of Italian descent, who still lives in Davis, said that her Father came from Italy around 1907. He, like many others who could not speak English, was given a sign to wear with the name of his destination printed on it in English to ensure that he got off at the correct depot— Davis, West Virginia.

The parents of Frances Tekavec, an 83-year resident of Davis, were Slovenian and came by steamship to Ellis Island. Ms. Tekavec was actually born in a timber camp at Laneville, near Dolly Sods. Her father drove a team of horses that hauled newly cut trees from the woods to a sawmill in Laneville.

Her mother worked along with other women as a cook for the camp. She would be at work by 3:30 in the morning in order to help prepare 80 to 100 loaves of bread, piles of flapjacks, eggs, meat and pies. The eighty "wood-hicks" had to be kept well fueled for their ten hour day of hand-sawing huge trees and cutting them into manageable lengths for transport to the mills. An eight-hour work-day would have been an impossible dream for them.

Ms. Tekavec spoke with incredible clarity

about how her family lived in a little two-room shanty near the camp, and a way of life incredibly different from that experienced today. These company owned shanties were the egalitarian-model of the modern mobile home. With a large hook embedded in the roof, the house could be easily hoisted by a winch and loaded onto a flatbed-railroad car. In this manner, the household could be moved to the next camp when the timber had been worked out of an area.

When she was six years old, her family moved to Camp Number Eight. It was located at the southern end of Davis, near the Rt. 32 bridge which crosses over the Blackwater River. Ms. Tekavec started public school a few years later when she was eight years old. She learned to speak English while playing with other children and from her public school teachers, whom she remembers as very kind and helpful in teaching the immigrant children how to speak English.

For the most part, people worked and lived together peacefully in spite of the language and cultural differences. It must have been a challenging but exciting life. The Catholics socialized and went to church together, as did the Methodists, Episcopalians and Baptists. During the early years before churches were built, the different congregations met in the town hall, or even in the company buildings. The small African American community was kept segregated much as everywhere else in America, having their own separate school and church.

In the midst of this remarkable, thriving community, hatred and racism reared their ugly heads. Ms. Tekavec recalls with an uncharacteristic shudder about the brief visits of the Klu Klux Klan to Davis. She and most other residents did not know the identity of the Klan members for they appeared in their infamous cone-shaped white hoods when demonstrating. She vividly recalls the pall of uncertainty and fear that gripped the community on the night the Klansmen burned a cross on the hill across from where the Bank of Davis is located.

She also remembers hearing about the "Pest House," located where route 93 intersects route 32 just north of town. In the early days of the community, people with serious communicable diseases were confined or quarantined in the Pest House until they recovered. Food was delivered from a local restaurant and left outside the door. A guard took the food in and distributed it to the patients. Many of those who went in, died in the house, but several individuals recovered and lived long lives after regaining their freedom. By 1907, the town had a physician and the pest house was closed. People with communicable diseases were then quarantined at home.

The town of Davis continually expanded throughout this economic boom. In 1902, it had a population of 3,000 people and nearly 80 businesses. A good majority of these enterprises included boarding houses, even private homeowners rented rooms to the migratory timber cutters. Over the next ten years, Davis acquired several large Victorian style homes, an opera house, two banks, two elegant hotels, three butcher shops, two bakeries, three doctors, two dentists, three lawyers and seven churches.

The Worden Hotel stood until the late 1970's when it closed and was disassembled. Many tourists and naturalists who traveled to the area to explore the unique ecosystem in Canaan Valley or those who came to ski, have fond memories of the once fine old hotel. There was an elaborate bar in this hotel, which is currently housed in *Grandpa's Attic* craft shop, located in the old Babcock Company Store near the bank. The proprietors of this shop love to show it off, and have lots of good stories to go with it, too.

Davis, West Virginia was one of the first towns in the state to have electricity. Thomas B. Davis, brother of Henry Gassaway Davis, and several other prominent business moguls including Fairfax S. Landstreet and Harry G. Buxton formed the Davis Electric Light Company. They built a dam on Beaver Creek to create a source of water to run the generators that created enough electricity for street lights and for the homes of those who could afford it.

From the time the major businesses started closing around 1918 until the Babcock operation ceased in 1924, the economic scenario in Davis remained consistently in a downward spiral until the present. Since 1924, the population in Davis has continued to diminish. Many of the families who remained found employment in the surrounding coal mining industries, or further away in Maryland. In the most recent years, most nearby industries have closed. Young people rarely stay in the area after high school graduation.

The acres of huge factory buildings and mills were torn down, and the materials loaded on railroad cars to be reconstructed for new enterprises elsewhere. Many of the beautiful Victorian buildings including a hotel, a theater and the wonderful hospital were disassembled for the same reason. The companies not only took the timber and coal, they took the best of what had been the structural foundations of the town. Though most of the buildings are gone, there is much to discover in Davis, and best of all, wonderful people to get to know.

Blackwater Falls State Park: Hope For A Struggling Town

In the late 1920's owners of the Blackwater Manor Tract sold their land to West Virginia Power and Transmission, setting the stage for the future environmental and economic conflicts that have come to define this region. When the land was purchased, the power company developed plans to construct a dam for a hydroelectric project across the Blackwater Canyon. This idea was never acted on due to the cost of such a project, and mostly because of the overwhelming attraction the falls and canyon of the Blackwater River has had for tourists.

Beginning in the late 1800's, the residents of Davis walked a 1½ mile-long trail to the falls for family recreation. To allow easy access to the falls, local residents built stone steps down to the falls. Families from surrounding communities also used the cleared site where the Dobbin House had stood for outings. Since the first human being came upon its splashing waters, the Blackwater River has been a magnet for those desiring scenic beauty in a natural setting.

The power company sold a portion of the original Blackwater Manor Tract to the United States Government in 1922 to become a part of the Monongahela National Forest. This purchase included land on the plateau on either side of the canyon. The power company held firmly to approximately 6000 acres, knowing that some future development opportunities would arise. Protection of the full length of the canyon would have more thoroughly benefited the watershed

Main Falls of the Blackwater River

of the Cheat River further downstream and added to the ecological integrity of the Monongahela National Forest lands.

In 1934, West Virginia Power and Transmission granted a temporary lease of 446 acres around Blackwater Falls for a state park. Asbury Cleaver, a resident of Davis and former timber worker became the caretaker. So many people came to the falls on weekends, that his major duty was directing traffic. At the present time, the roads can adequately handle the vehicular traffic. But on a beautiful fall weekend, you have to stand in line on the boardwalk and elbow your way to a clear view, before you can take a picture of the falls. Unlike the day-after-Thanksgiving department store lines, people are smiling, serene and uplifted.

Blackwater Falls was officially brought into the State Park System in 1937 at the height of the Great Depression. Men from the Civilian Conservation Corps planted thousands of trees in the "boulder fields" around Davis and within the park boundaries. In many places, they had to haul in buckets of soil from Canaan Valley in order to give the seedlings a "shot" of organic matter. The bogs bordering the road between Pendleton Lake and the main park road is one such area that did not receive any intensive restoration. Soil development has only within the last few decades advanced to a state where trees have begun to get a foothold.

In 1953 West Virginia Power and Transmission deeded 935 acres to the state for the park. The following year, several planned improvements to the park had been drafted including the lodge, playground areas, cabins, and campground, stables and picnic areas. The park got its first superintendent in 1955. In 1957, the beautiful stone and wood, 55-room lodge was completed. The restaurant in the lodge has a seating capacity of 250 people and magnificent views of the canyon. During that same year the State Park System and Monongahela National Forest made a land swap, and 744 acres of land was added to Blackwater Falls State Park. Since that year, the park has only moderately increased its facilities, retaining the natural wildness around which it was formed.

Blackwater Lodge

Geologic History
(Where Did All
Those Rocks Come From?)

Blackwater Falls State Park lies within a region once referred to as "Canada." The vegetation of the high-elevated plateau rimmed from horizon to horizon with dark-green-spires of spruce trees, interspersed with open sphagnum bogs was the inspiration for this analogy. The name was also meant to distinguish the plateau region from Canaan Valley. However, we now know that the two areas are inextricably linked by a shared geologic history, and by the waters of one river.

Along the southern rim of Blackwater Falls State Park at 3200 feet in elevation, the land ascends slowly and gently another 500 feet in elevation to a patchwork of bogs and spruce stands across the top of Canaan Mountain. From the eastern rim of Canaan Mountain you can peer down a steep, 600-foot elevation descent into the thirteen miles long, three to five mile wide basin of Canaan Valley.

Blackwater River rises in the southwestern end of Canaan Valley and meanders northwestward for a short distance, turning sharply to a more northeastward direction near Canaan Valley State Park. Throughout the remaining length of Canaan Valley, the river continues its northeasterly flow. This orientation of the stream bed in the valley has an opposite direction of flow and yet is parallel to the stream bed through Blackwater Falls State Park. Essentially, the river makes a giant horseshoe-shape around Canaan Mountain.

As the river emerges from Canaan Valley, cutting a gap between Canaan and Brown Mountains, it arcs to the west, winding westerly through low marshy ground till it reaches the town of Davis, West Virginia. Just below Davis, the river turns to the south to flow in a southwestward direction through Blackwater Falls State Park. Once it careens over the falls it continues in a southwestward direction to the mouth of the river at Hendricks.

This amazing little river only 30.6 miles long carved both the broad-level bowl of Canaan Valley and the deep, precipitous Blackwater Canyon. To make this scenario even more intriguing, the rocks exposed in Canaan Valley are much older than those forming the canyon walls further downstream and at a much lower elevation.

The old saying "there is nothing new under the sun" could be a geologist's creed. For the plateau supporting the park was once a sea, the boulders in the canyon were once sediments eroded from an ancient, extinct mountain system, every molecule of water, and every atom of carbon in the trees were all part of something else, many times over since the earth was formed. The earth is one giant recycling bin!

To explain how the rocks you see in Blackwater Falls State Park were formed, we need to look way back in geologic time. There are about four major geologic events or processes that unfolded over millions of years, shaping the current landscape. These events are listed in the order of occurrence below.

1. Period of sediment deposition and rock formation
2. Period of mountain building, uplift and folding of thousands of layers of rock
3. Erosion of mountains to a hilly plain, with some continued uplift
4. Downward cutting of streams into rock layers with no uplift

The first period began 600 million years ago. From 600 million years ago, until approximately 230 million years ago, this region was part of a deep basin. The basin was repeatedly inundated from the west by shallow seas. A massive mountain range extended along what is now the eastern seaboard during this period. Eon after eon, sediments eroded from the mountains to the east and were washed into and settled in the basin.

During this 370 million year deposition phase, streams flowed from the mountains carrying various types of sediments. The kinds of sediments deposited were influenced by the environmental conditions at the time. Microscopic organisms made limestone deposits when the seas filled the basin. These limestone deposits would be buried under hundreds of feet of alternating layers of sand and silt as the rivers and streams poured into the sea from the mountains. We can see the same process occurring today where sediment-laden rivers wash into the oceans.

From 345 million years ago to 330 million years ago (early Mississippian Period) the salt-water seas retreated to the west and fresh-water streams deposited red shale and sandstone. The seas came back 330 million years ago and covered the region until 310 million years ago. During this portion of the Mississippian Period, vast limestone beds were deposited. At the end of this period the red shale of the Mauch Chunk Group exposed along the upper rim of Canaan Valley were formed.

From 310 million years ago until 280 million years ago the seas were gone and vast swamps dominated the region. Thousands of feet of peat accumulated during the millions of years when the swamps were present. Many of the most important coal seams were formed during this time period, which represents the early part of the Pennsylvanian Period.

Geologists have determined that the deposits accumulated over these millions of years equaled about eight miles in thickness. Around 230 million years ago the deposition of material ended in this region, culminating the first of the four major events. At this epoch juncture, give or take a few million years, a dramatic period of mountain building began.

The tectonic plate supporting the North American Continent began colliding with the tectonic plate carrying the African Continent. This collision occurred forcefully, but slowly, over the span of several million years. As the continents were relentlessly pushed together, the thousands of feet of horizontal rock layers resulting from the 370-million-year deposition phase were folded, buckled, bent and/or broken.

The entire rock-and-sediment-filled basin was uplifted during this mountain building phase. The land mass was lifted higher in the northeast than it was toward the southwest. The rocks in the east closer to the compression force were more significantly folded and bent. The mountains that were created are thought to have been as high or higher than the current Himalayan Mountains.

At the end of the mountain building, the erosion phase began; it represents the third marker. The mountain peaks were eroded to a nearly level plain several times. After, and sometimes during each leveling period, the land was uplifted and the existing streams were able to cut deeper into the plateau of rock.

The fourth segment of this geologic saga has been unfolding over the last 60 to 70 million years. It has been a period of downward stream cutting with no uplift. The canyon and Canaan Valley as they appear today have resulted from this continual erosive action of the streams coupled with the forces of harsh winter freezing and thawing of ice in every crack and fissure of the rocks. If this trend were to continue for many millions of years the Blackwater Canyon would eventually become a broad valley with a slow moving river.

The chart on Page 93 showing a cross section of the rock strata underlying Blackwater Falls State Park and Canaan Valley, may more clearly demonstrate the geology of the region. Rocks that were folded during the mountain building phase underlie both parks. Notice the undulating shape of the rock layers underlying the region. Blackwater River has cut into a syncline (downward warp of the underlying rock), while Canaan Valley occurs on an anticline (upward warp of the underlying rock).

The pattern of erosion and landforms created are the result of climatic factors and the rock type subjected to weathering. Sandstone rock is quite resistant to weathering. Softer shale is more easily eroded and limestone rock is subjected to chemical weathering.

When anticlines are folded upward, cracks occur in the top allowing water to seep into the underlying rocks. By looking at the diagram you can see that the Conemaugh, Allegheny and Pottsville sandstones were removed by erosion from Canaan Valley. Only the Pottsville sandstone is left around the rim of the valley. Cracks and breaks in these weather-resistant layers resulting from the folding, allowed them to be broken down and carried away.

Also observe how the upward sloping of the rocks under Canaan Valley explains why older rock strata are exposed at the surface in Canaan Valley than in the gorge section of Blackwater River. The very hard, weather resistant Pocono Sandstone underlies the Blackwater River in Canaan Valley. This rock layer has nearly stopped the down cutting of the river in this area. That is why the stream flows slowly, in wide sweeping arcs.

Look at the list of rock strata underlying Blackwater Falls State Park. Notice that the layers exposed in the canyon are primarily composed of softer shale and coal. The presence of the softer rocks explains the more rapid down cutting of the river and the formation of the canyon. The softer rocks were exposed to the year-round forces of erosion once the river broke through the resistant Connoquenessing Sandstone.

The Upper Connoquenessing sandstone is the rock strata forming the 57-foot falls. The forty-foot cliff above the falls is also composed of the same type of rock. It is a highly weather-resistant sandstone. However, in time, the falls will slowly cut away at the rock, moving the ledge further and further upstream. Some future version of Homo sapiens, say two million years from now, will have to go to Canaan Valley to see the Falls of the Blackwater River.

When you look into the canyon from any one of the overlooks in the park, notice the numerous rock cliffs jutting from the canyon wall and the huge boulders lining the riverbed. These rock caps represent erosion-resistant layers of sandstone.

You cannot escape the presence of rocks anywhere in Blackwater Falls State Park. The rock layers just under the soil and exposed around the canyon rim are made of sandstone. When the timber was cut at the turn of the century and soil burned away, the underlying rock layers were exposed to physical and chemical weathering.

The seventy to eighty years that the vegetation has had to regenerate has not been nearly enough time to break down the rocks. Nor has the soil been able to accumulate to a depth that would cover the fragmented rock base in this high elevation, harsh-climate environment. The resistant sandstone rocks covering the park will take hundreds, perhaps thousands of years to decay.

The interminable sea of sandstone ruble littering the forest floor throughout Blackwater Falls State Park has at least provided a supply of anchors for the struggling birch, hemlock, beech and other tree species. The expansive network of sprawling tree roots and rocks have created beautiful shapes and sculptures as these two foundations of the current forest bond for life. This web of rocks and roots braided through by countless streams is a metaphor for the basic ecological principle that "everything in nature is interconnected."

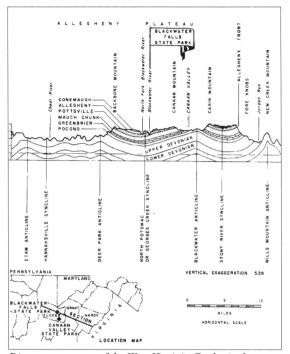

Diagram courtesy of the West Virginia Geological Survey

Selected Hiking Trails
Blackwater Falls State Park

Fourteen miles of hiking trails loop and criss-cross into a network within the 1,688 acres of Blackwater Falls State Park. The trails discussed below list those easily accessed from the lodge first, followed by those accessed from the Pendleton Lake parking lot.

The mileage given for each trail represents a one-way distance. Most of the trails are about a mile or less in length. You can create your own loop hike where the various trails intersect. The most difficult aspect of all of the trails in Blackwater Falls State Park is the presence of rocks and boulders. Use the following criterion for choosing trails.

> I - Easy grade and can be walked by most anyone; normal street shoes appropriate
> I-C – Easy grade, but some caution required due to the presence of exposed tree roots and boulders along the trail. May not be suitable for very young children or those with difficulty walking
> II. - Moderate grade; some rock hopping; hiking boots or shoes recommended. Average fitness acceptable
> III. - Relatively steep in places; hiking boots and good physical condition recommended

Trails on both sides of the Blackwater River Canyon connect with the Monongahela National Forest trail system, significantly extending your hiking/skiing opportunities. It is possible to begin a backpack trip into the Monongahela National Forest from Blackwater Falls State Park up onto Canaan Mountain, and return to your destination without backtracking.

Trails in Blackwater Falls State Park and those connecting with the Monongahela National Forest System are well blazed and easy to follow, spring through winter. Approximately 12 miles of trails in Blackwater Falls State Park are suitable for cross-country skiing.

Check with the Park Naturalist for cross-country skiing information, for individual maps of the Monongahela National Forest Trails on Canaan Mountain and trails in the Dobbin House Loop System. Bikes are prohibited on trails unless indicted otherwise.

Trails Accessible From Blackwater Lodge:

ELAKALA TRAIL

Elakala Trail is a one-half mile trace that begins just outside the recreation room of the lodge. It follows the canyon rim of Shay Run to the Park Road across from the Balanced Rock Trail. The trail is marked with a red circle blaze. Difficulty II. No cross-country skiing allowed.

Elakala may be the most popular and well-worn trail in Blackwater Falls State Park. It is accessible to most hikers in spite of the rugged canyon it circumvents and is short enough to hike in less than one hour. In the early morning or late evening hours, Elakala Trail yields a remarkable retreat from the din of modern life into a mysterious world of sculpted rocks, splashing water, sprawling ferns and mosses and wonderfully melodious birds.

Immerse your senses in the range of nature's music as you cross the sturdy wooden beam bridge over Elakala Falls of Shay Run. Water splashes down the terraces above the bridge and careens over the steep cliff below, creating a cacophony of water sounds. The interlocking branches of hemlock trees shade the stream as the surreal songs of the veery and winter wren echo from the depths below. Exposed roots of yellow birch and hemlock trees snake over and around the boulders on the steep banks ahead, creating inviting cavities for exploration.

Monstrous boulders heavily coated with lichens and mosses litter the canyon wall above and below the trail. The rock walls towering above Shay Run, misted by water spewing from the spray of the falls are wet and thickly matted with several species of mosses, ferns and liverworts. The annual average rainfall in the Allegheny Mountains is higher than in any other part of West Virginia. The higher rainfall coupled with year-round low cloud cover makes an ideal

Elakala Trail

Drawing by David Hunter Strother from The
Blackwater Chronicle *by John Pendleton Kennedy, 1853
New York*

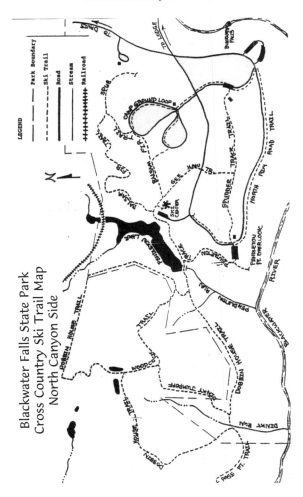

Blackwater Falls State Park
Cross Country Ski Trail Map
North Canyon Side

environment for plants like lichens and mosses which have no internal plumbing to transport water from one part of the plant to another. These plants must intake most of the water they need by direct contact with atmospheric moisture and/or rain water.

Here in Blackwater Falls State Park, mosses cover wide stretches of the forest floor particularly under conifer stands. Mosses cover living and dead trees, fill in the bogs and carpet the rocks along Elakala Trail. They play a vital role in stabilizing the slowly accumulating soil, by absorbing rainwater and preventing soil erosion. Decaying mosses provide a good portion of the organic matter incorporated into

Elakala Falls on Elakala Trail

the soil. Despite their ecological importance, mosses have been little studied in this area.

Amphibians are a group of small animals that thrive in this habitat. Amphibians, like the kinds of plants dominating the forest floor are an ancient, primitive group of organisms. Several species of salamanders have been identified from this watershed and throughout the surrounding region. But you will have to come out at night to see them, salamanders are primarily nocturnal in their feeding, and remain in burrows under rocks and logs during the day.

In spite of their tiny size and humble life, there is nothing primitive about the role and value that salamanders have in the ecosystem. Dr. Tom Pauley, an expert on West Virginia's salamanders and reptiles, discovered that salamanders occur in dense numbers in West Virginia's forests, feeding on a host of insects and worms. They act as nature's tillers by turning the soil thus helping to distribute organic matter throughout the soil. As many as ten or eleven species may be found in the canyon above and below Elakala Trail.

Cheat Mountain salamander

Dr. Pauley has co-authored with the late Dr. N. Bayard Green a wonderful book, *Amphibians & Reptiles In West Virginia,* on the biology and distribution of salamanders and reptiles within the state. Through his work, Dr. Pauley discovered separate populations of the threatened Cheat Mountain salamander on either side of Elakala Trail. His studies have shown that salamanders from the distinct populations do not cross the trail.

Salamanders have been found to be declining in numbers throughout the world. Scientists are working hard to find out why. The decline of these animals may be due to some environmental problem that could ultimately have negative effects on people. Understanding the fate of these little creatures living secretively and unknown to most who walk here, reminds us of those prophetic words spoken by John Muir, "When we try to pick out anything by itself, we find it hitched to everything else in the universe." Though we may not entirely understand why, we are hitched to these little creatures.

If you decide to look under rocks for salamanders, be sure and return all rocks and logs to their original position in order to protect the natural habitat that these and other animals depend on. Also, never remove any animals from the location where you found them. Especially in a park, where so many people visit the same places, it is essential that we minimally disturb the animals and plants so as to not place undue stress on the ecosystem.

Elakala Trail hugs the wall of the ravine as it traverses a fairly straight line away from the bridge. Near the end of the trail you will have to descend a few stairs and then climb up a relatively steep, but sturdy wooden staircase for fifteen feet or so. From this point, the trail climbs gently to the main Park Road.

DAVIS TRAIL

Canaan/Blackwater Trail

Within the park boundary Davis Trail is only about one-quarter mile long, difficulty I. It can be accessed from the parking lot at the Riding Stables or from the Yellow Birch Trail. The full length of this trail is about 2.8 miles as it gradually ascends Canaan Mountain to the Canaan Loop Road (CLR) on top. Davis Trail is marked with a white circle blaze and the blue triangular blaze of the long-distance Allegheny Trail that is concurrent with Davis Trail for a while. About mid-way, Davis Trail intersects Plantation Trail that runs east to west completely bisecting the Canaan Loop Road.

A challenging 6.5 mile long loop hike can be made by taking Davis Trail from the stables until it intersects Plantation Trail (approx. 1.6 miles). Turn Right onto Plantation Trail and walk till it intersects Lindy Run Trail (approx. 2 miles). Turn right onto Lindy Run and follow it to the CLR (approx. 1 mile) where you will turn right to walk back into the park and follow the road or pick up a series of trails which parallel the road to the Riding Stables (approx. 2 miles). This loop will take you through a variety of vegetation patterns and along some beautiful streams. Intermediate to advance cross-country skiing. Bicycles permitted. Difficulty III

The first half-mile of Davis Trail is a gentle walk along an old railroad bed built along Engine Run. The waters of this wide stream tumble and splash over and around large boulders. Quartzite crystals of varying shades from pink to alabaster line the stream bed. Brilliant-green sphagnum moss fills in the bogs beside the trail. This section of Davis Trail is lined with lush colonies of rhododendron. Mountain laurel bushes peek out from under ruffled-skirts of the larger protective-cover of rhododendrons.

Yellow birch, hemlock and spruce tower above the shrubs on the gradually ascending land on either side of the trail. The ground under the trees and along the edges of the trail is covered with Lycopodium, mosses and lichens. Thick mats of unusual species of mosses line the banks of Engine Run and choke the tiny bogs along the trail. Velvet leaf blueberry shrubs occur in patches in the bogs. In the fall, when the leaves on all the heaths turn red, this section of the trail is spectacular. Eventually the trail becomes a little steeper as it veers away from Engine Run. Near where the trail crosses Plantation Trail you will see a little path leading to a six-person shelter.

From the riding stables, Davis Trail is also a starting point for the 8 ½ mile Canaan/ Blackwater Cross Country Ski Trail. It is known as the *Trail Between The Parks* because you can walk from the Riding Stables in Blackwater to the Lodge area in Canaan Valley State Park. While hiking this trail, you can experience the crystal waters of Engine Run; climb through a young hardwood stand and then through a red spruce plantation to the top of Canaan Mountain. On Canaan Mountain, the trail passes through cranberry bogs and a rich hardwood forest down the slopes of the mountain. Lodge guests staying at either park can usually arrange for a shuttle back to their car with park personnel. You need to check at the office in either park in order to make arrangements.

SHAY TRACE

Shay Trace is approximately three-quarters of a mile long. It is marked with a blue circle blaze. You may begin along the main road across from the Upper Lodge entrance or behind the Warming Hut on the other end. This trail crosses Red Spruce Riding Trail, the Cabin Road and Cherry Lane Trail. Difficulty II. Intermediate to advance cross-country skiing.

Shay Trace is a lovely, wide meander through maturing woods over an old Babcock Boom and Lumber Company railroad grade. On one end, the trail winds through a grove of northern hardwoods near the cabin area but eventually weaves through a young sub alpine spruce forest.

The ground is carpeted with several species of Lycopodium and mosses. In some places a dense carpet of a Lycopodium called tree clubmoss, covers the ground at an even height. The name Lycopodium is derived from two Greek words, *lycos* meaning wolf, and *pous*, foot, thus wolf foot. This relates to the spreading, hairy appearance of the leaves on some species.

The powdery, microscopic spores produced on these plants have a long history of use in folklore medicine and even into modern times has been found to have several uses. The powdery spores have a low flash point, and were used for years as flash powder in the first cameras. Fireworks were often ignited with the aid of the powdery spores. And, druggists would scatter the powder among pills to keep them dry and separated.

Some tree species that you will see near the cabin area include American beech, red maple, black cherry, yellow birch and hemlock. Once you descend away from this upland area the forest changes to spruce, hemlock and birch, typical of the developing sub alpine habitat seen along Yellow Birch Trail, Red Spruce and Stemwinder riding trails.

Much of this area was originally covered

Shay Trace Trail

with a true sub alpine or mixed red spruce and hardwoods forest. Dr. Kenneth Carvell, retired forestry professor and noted West Virginia historian shared an interesting story about the fate of some of the former giant spruce processed at the sawmills in Davis. Apparently, not all of it went into making paper.

> "Between 1880 and 1930 everyone (who was anyone) bought a piano. (It was a status symbol…you had arrived socially.) Everyone knew that the sounding boards came from spruce from the far north, due to the spruce's good resonating qualities. Piano manufacturers were depleting suitable material from the north, and were interested in West Virginia spruce, but were reluctant to use it, as West Virginia was considered by most to be a southern state.
>
> The first freight cars carrying red spruce from West Virginia arrived at the piano factories (Baltimore, New York, Philadelphia and Boston) in unmarked cars. Within in a short time, it had proven so superior to the northern spruce (wider boards, free from blemish and defect), that later not only did the freight cars say *West Virginia Spruce* but every board was

surcharged *West Virginia Spruce*." If you have an old piano, manufactured from sometime between 1880 and 1930, it probably has a *West Virginia Spruce* sounding board.

There are the usual moss-covered boulder fields stretching across the forest floor. Small pockets of sphagnum bogs occur among the boulders. Creeping snowberry occurs in at least one location along the trail. Large hemlocks and red spruce trees create a deep woods atmosphere in a few intermittent sections where Lycopodium spread across the ground in very dense patches.

Under the shade of hemlocks and spruce, dead trees are covered with carpet moss. The moss is so thick and expansive across some of these trees it appears to be like a snug-fitting green cloak. One tree in particular evokes the image drawn by Rebecca Harding Davis of "a dead body, which undisturbed in the slow passage of uncounted years, had made all this false show of life." In the spring, look for isolated plants of painted trillium and Canada mayflower.

The section of the trail from the warming hut is fairly level and lined with some large hemlocks and large colonies of rhododendron. Look for tulip poplar, striped maple, yellow birch, red maple, and beech as well. Rhododendron occurs in several places along the trail. A wide expanse of gently sloping woodlands spreads before you as you enter this trail from the warming hut.

The section of the trail closer to the lodge passes by a large sandstone cliff covered with mosses and rock tripe lichen. Rhododendron and mountain laurel grow in abundance at this location as well. The trail descends gently through the mixed conifer and hardwoods forest to cross Shay Run over a sturdy wooden-beam bridge before ending at the hard-topped road.

YELLOW BIRCH TRAIL

Distance: 1-½ miles. Marked with a yellow circle blaze. Difficulty 2. Main trailhead across from entrance to the lodge, The trail meanders through woods parallel to the main park road to cross the stable entrance road and continues on to the maintenance area road. Hikers may cross the Park Road to the Gentle Trail, then return by the road or by the same trail. Difficulty II.

There is not a habitat in Blackwater Falls State Park entirely devoid of yellow birch trees. Though the scattered hemlock and red spruce trees sometimes dwarf their presence, yellow birch is fairly abundant on this trail. Particularly in the winter, the dark green evergreens outshine the dull yellowish bark of yellow birch and the grayish color of the red maples and other species.

Winding in a serpentine narrow swath through tall trees and brushy patches, this trail allows a true woodlands experience in contrast to the wider trails of the park. Despite the relatively level nature of Yellow Birch Trail, it is not that easy to walk. The base of the trail is littered with huge, jagged stones of the Homewood formation. Just as in other areas of the park, the shallow soil leaves the larger, supporting roots of the trees exposed across the surface.

I would especially recommend walking this trail in the early morning or late evening, to avoid the interruption of the sounds of cars traveling the park road below the trail. However, in a few places the trail winds far enough away from the Park Road to escape the noises of human activity.

Be not deterred by a few rocks and wet places, wear sturdy walking shoes and approach Yellow Birch Trail with an adventurous spirit. Within the dark denizens where spruce and hemlock branches filter the sunlight, let your imagination take wild flights of fancy to the days of those intrepid surveyors seeking the "fountain head" of the Potomac, or the swashbuckling adventure seekers of the Blackwater Expedition. This section of woods truly merits the distinction of a sub alpine forest.

Emerging from crevices between the boulders and along the base of trees intermediate wood ferns spread their showy dark green foliage. During the winter months these ferns will lie prostrate on the ground, flattened by the heavy snows. This is one of the few fern species to remain green all year.

Portions of the trail go through more brushy areas where the tree canopy is lower and the rhododendron colonies more dispersed. Several patches of rhododendrons are dead or dying in these areas. However, the section of the trail beginning at the Horse Stables passes through dense rhododendron thickets. You will also have to climb over a huge sandstone boulder. The trail winds through a gap in this rock formation, making the passage relatively fun, but not dangerous.

About a quarter-mile from the trailhead near Gentle Trail, Yellow Birch Trail crosses a small stream where a sphagnum/cranberry bog has developed along its banks. Cranberry plants are trailing plants with tiny, evergreen leaves that look somewhat like a patch of trailing hemlock branches. Watch for the rose-colored flowers in June or early July and the ripe cranberries in September. The name cranberry comes from the shape of the flowers which early people thought resembled the beak of a crane.

This is one of the more lovely, and isolated spots in the park, and it truly looks and feels like the Canada that the early explorers compared this region to. The native ranges of the sundew, cranberry, cottongrass, sphagnum moss and other plants that grow here occur as far north as Newfoundland. Some ecologists consider these plants to be "relict" species, isolated from their natural latitudinal range. The unique geologic and climatic factors which produce the bogs, are the elements that allow these plants to be here.

Sphagnum moss, which is so common throughout the park, is a type of peat moss. It grows in thick mats in this bog, and also occurs beside streams and in bogs all over the park. When allowed to grow undisturbed for centuries, vast beds of partially decayed sphagnum accumulate as peat. Peat is commercially harvested all over the world to be sold as mulch.

In much of Northern Europe, huge blocks of peat have been dug from bogs to be dried and used as a fuel when the supply of fossil fuels runs low. Coal is formed when hundreds and even thousands of feet of peat have been buried by sediment and altered by the resulting heat and pressure.

Wet sphagnum has been used for thousands of years as an antiseptic bandage. Even as late as World War I, sphagnum moss was used to treat battle wounds when the supply of cotton bandages was low. The antiseptic properties of the plant actually made it a better bandage than the cotton bandages, especially when the cotton bandages were not kept sterile.

Also look for creeping snowberry, a very uncommon plant found only in cold, mossy woods and bogs of the northern latitudes. It is similar in form to cranberry, except that the individual leaflets along the stem are oval and tipped with tiny points. The urn-shaped, four-millimeter long flowers

Cranberry Bog off Yellow Birch Trail

appear singly in the leaf axils around the middle of May. The flowers produce white, aromatic berries toward the end of summer.

Snowberry, cranberry, rhododendron and mountain laurel share a common ancestry. These plants are all members of the heath family. The characteristics they share include alternate leaves, flowers with 4 to 5 petals, often fused, fruit is a many-seeded berry and all require thin acidic soils, or bog-like environments. Rhododendrons and mountain laurels can grow on dry, desert-like sandstone rocks with very little soil, or along streams with sandstone base.

Cotton-grass also grows in the bog—it is slightly misnamed for it is actually a sedge, another of the boreal species found only in isolated bogs throughout West Virginia. Extensive patches of it grow in Canaan Valley. Cottongrass produces a long, wiry stem and similar looking leaves. In July, a beautiful tuft-like seed head occurs at the top of the plant that looks like a ball of cotton from a distance. The puffy wands persist through late summer and fall, but will be flattened by the first snows. Flower heads may appear yellowish or brownish.

Probably the most stunning plant to occur in this little bog is round-leaved sundew, which grows throughout the bog. These 1 to 2 inch wide plants glisten like rubies in the sun and are

Bog on Yellow Birch Trail

easy to spot. Several reddish-green, spoon-shaped leaves radiate outward from a central axis. Each leaf is covered with upright glandular hairs that secrete a sticky fluid of digestive enzymes. The fragrance of the fluid attracts insects much as nectar does. However once an insect lands on the leaf, it becomes stuck in the fluid. The leaf-arms then bend inward trapping and digesting the insect over a 24-to 48-hour period.

Sundew plants are common in only a few bogs throughout West Virginia. They are delicate plants and would not survive being trampled. It is best to remain on the boardwalk crossing over the bog and enjoy its beauty from a location that will leave it protected. You may skirt through the woods along the edge of the bog to get a closer look at the plants and habitat. Notice the number of spruce and hemlock tree seedlings and saplings scattered across the bog. As they increase in size and number, the trees will change the character of the bog. However, it will be many, many years before this happens.

Further along the trail, watch for the "octopus birch." The roots of this particular tree appear to be the arms of a huge octopus standing on their tips with the massive tree trunk resting on the head of the octopus. The ability of these trees to thrive in such an inhospitable environment is amazing. A few grains of weathered rock, a patch of decayed moss, lots of water and a steady stream of photons were all that was needed to manufacture these tree statues that stimulate and delight our imaginations.

BALANCED ROCK TRAIL

A one mile, one-way trail. Orange circle blaze. Access Balanced Rock Trail along the main park road across from Elakala Trail. Balanced Rock Trail crosses Shay Trace and Red Spruce Riding Trail to the balanced rock, located below cabin 13. Difficulty II. Intermediate to advance cross-country skiing.

Balanced Rock Trail passes through similar habitats through which Shay Trace and Cherry

Lane Trails traverse. The forest is a mix of red spruce, yellow birch, red maple, beech and hemlock. There appears to be more of an understory in places where seedlings of red spruce, hemlock and young striped maple trees fill in the void of space under the canopy.

As of this writing, the orange blaze marks on the trees are very faint. The trail is narrow, but is easy to follow due to the consistent use this trail receives. However, in the fall after the leaves have fallen and before there is any snow on the ground, Balanced Rock Trail is a little more difficult to follow, so pay close attention. **Also, at a point about mid-way going towards the Balanced Rock from the road, the trail makes a sharp loop to the left that is not well marked**.

There are expansive colonies of rhododendron and mountain laurel sheltering the trail. The trail goes up-hill away from the stream and passes through a fairly dense rhododendron grove. Mountain holly is very common along this trail. Look for a small tree with warty-gray-bark and growing as a colony of multiple stems. Mountain holly is one of only two species of deciduous hollies. The berries this tree produces are valuable for wildlife. Other trees that characterize mountain habitats on this trail include mountain ash and serviceberry.

The balanced rock itself is beginning to disappear behind expanding branches of mountain holly and rhododendron. The trail winds up onto and around the back of a large sandstone boulder that appears to be balanced on top of a smaller one. It is a very lovely walk through a pattern of alternating patches of open and dense vegetation. To make a loop, walk back a short distance from the balanced rock to intersect with the Rhododendron Trail and follow it back to Cabin 13. Walk down the cabin road to the head of Shay Trace and then follow it back to the main park road and on to Blackwater Lodge.

Rhododendron Trail is a half-mile trail through the same mixed hemlock and hard-woods forest as Balanced Rock Trail. Rhododendron serves to connect the Cabin area with Balanced Rock Trail and all the other connecting trails in this area.

Drawing by John Northeimer, courtesy of the Division of Tourism & Parks

Trails Accessed From The Cabin Area

CHERRY LANE TRAIL

Cherry Lane Trail may be accessed at the end of the Cabin Area. A one-mile long trail makes a loop through a stand of northern hardwoods. It has a fairly easy grade with very little uphill or down hill walking. Intermediate to advance cross-country skiing. Difficulty level I.

Beginning at the end of the cabin area, walk out the wide road past the sled run to enter a cathedral-like hardwoods forest. Notice the resourcefulness of the park management as you pass the machine running the towrope. The towrope device is attached to the engine of an old park truck.

Once you are just a hundred feet beyond the sled run, the beautiful northern hardwoods forest will captivate you. Beech, black cherry, red maple and yellow birch tower to a height of 80-90 feet over the Lycopodium and moss covered forest floor. The ground rises gently to the left of the trail while it descends in a wide-open expanse to your right. A few scattered hemlock stand like little sentinels guarding the serenity of the woodland.

Year-round you may be soothed by the wind whipping through the treetops high above you. The gleeful sounds of gurgling water emanate from a tiny stream as it trickles over rocks and boulders. Moss covered rocks of various sizes dot the forest floor adding a touch of green throughout winter and early spring.

Cherry Lane Trail ascends through the woods to a plateau where you will immediately find yourself surrounded by rhododendron on both sides of the trail. The rhododendron do not look healthy, in fact several stems are dead. In the winter, lower branches on the plants will be bare from where deer have browsed the leaves. The deer browsing may be contributing to the poor health of the rhododendron, but there may also be some fungal disease attacking them.

Throughout the winter and early spring months look for brown creepers, hairy woodpeckers, downy woodpeckers, black

Cherry Lane Trail

capped chickadees, tufted titmice and pileated woodpeckersm. During the summer you will see and hear black-throated green warblers, magnolia warblers, veery and winter wrens. One of the best places to watch for birds is along the edge of the sled run and the woods. Yellow-shafted flickers and robins may be seen looking for worms on the grassy sled-run.

Just to the right of Cherry Lane Trail is a lovely open bog. Pockets of standing water exist most of the year in between patches of higher ground upon which low shrubs and trees have become established. Mounds of Polytrichum moss have generated these raised places called hummocks (accumulated layers of decaying moss) that will keep your feet dry if you can hop from one to the other. Due to the year-round cold water and acidic conditions in the bogs, dead plants decay very slowly. This is why bogs thousands of years old will have hundreds of feet of accumulated peat.

Vines of hispid dewberry crawl across the glade in loose patches. Spreading clusters of the slender stems of mountain holly occur sporadically across the glade. Other plants that grow in isolated clusters across the open glade include mountain laurel, glade St. Johnswort, rhododendron, spruce seedlings and young hemlock. Blowing lightly in the continual breeze are the slender, whitish stems of thick patches of Danthonia grass. Danthonia is also called Allegheny flyback because the stems arch over and fly back even when pressed to remain upright.

The pointed tops of even-aged hemlock and spruce appear like the tips of a giant picket fence surrounding the glade. This is a magical place on a sunny day when the deep blue sky meets the dark green evergreens, and the vegetation on the floor of the glade takes on a golden cast. Occasionally, the silence is interrupted by the nasal squawk of a raven as it flies overhead or the squeaking noise of two trees rubbing against each other in the periodic gusts of wind that whip through the woods.

Beyond the glade, the trail once again meanders through a rambling seven to ten foot tall rhododendron colony. Thick roots of yellow birch trees splay across the trail in this area making it a little more difficult to walk without looking down. Beech trees become prominent again. Look for a few scattered witch hazel and tulip poplar trees. The ground is wet in this area and the park has provided birch-limb bridges to help you keep your feet dry as you complete the loop back through the woods to enter the Cabin Area again.

Lindy Point Trail

Lindy Point Trail is a newly constructed long easy grade from Canaan Loop Road out to Lindy Point Overlook. The trail is located one mile below the sled run on the right side of Canaan Loop Road. Look for a small parking area. Trail difficulty I.

The view of Blackwater River Canyon from Lindy Point Overlook has been one of the most photographed geologic features in West Virginia. A massive sandstone rock extends over the canyon, high above the confluence of Lindy Run and the Blackwater River. Standing on the flat surface of the rock outcrop you can see for miles upstream and downstream. The grayish-white rocks create a lovely contrast to the dark green vegetation all around it.

Lindy Point Trail carves a narrow tunnel through thickets of rhododendron and other trees. Then, without warning, the hiker emerges into a full view of the deep canyon below and a vast open sky as far as the eye can see. The tall trees and thick shrubs provide no clue of what lies head until the trail ends at the cliff.

Small-scattered openings provide an opportunity to see some interesting plants. About midway along the trail look for the large basal leaves of pink lady's slipper. Look for flattened-rosettes of the green and white checkered leaves of an orchid called rattlesnake plantain. This plant will produce a four to six inch stem with little white flowers in June. At least four different species of Lycopodium occur beside the trail as well.

As soon as funds are available, the whole trail will be covered with gravel.

Coming Down The Mountain,
Harper's New Monthly Magazine,
No. CCCLXII, July, 1880, Vol. LXI

COMING DOWN THE MOUNTAIN.

Trails Accessed From Pendleton Lake:

BALSAM FIR TRAIL

A 1.5-mile loop trail. Blue Circle Blaze. Difficulty I. This easily walked trail begins at the basketball court near the Recreation Building, winds through an open woodland to the campground area from where it loops back to the Recreation Building. Suitable for intermediate cross-country skiing.

Balsam Fir Trail provides a gentle walk through a small stand of conifers (trees with needle-like leaves) and a young beech forest.

Balsam Fir Trail

Balsam fir is a very uncommon species found naturally in only a few locations in the state. More than likely, CCC workers planted the few trees growing here. Balsam fir is found around the periphery of sphagnum bogs in Canaan Valley and was associated with the original red spruce forests, which once blanketed the higher elevations on Canaan Mountain. Balsam fir is a sub alpine species and reaches the southern most extent of its range in this area.

Before entering the conifer stand, the trail passes through a cluster of young black cherry and serviceberry trees, bordered by a noticeable tall shrub called smooth arrow-wood. This plant is an attractive member of the genus Viburnum. Arrow-wood has sharply toothed, nearly heart-shaped, opposite leaves. Spreading-heads of small white flowers are produced in May or June at the ends of branches on the 4 to 12 foot tall shrubs. Clusters of blue-black berries appear in late summer. These berries provide food for many species of birds.

This small stand of conifers also includes Scotch pine, Norway spruce and hemlock. The CCC workers planted most of these trees in the early 1930's as part of the forest restoration project begun as early as 1920 by employees of the Monongahela National Forest. Some of these trees are rather large, and create a cool shady retreat on a hot summer day.

Look closely at the needles on the conifers and you will notice that they have flattened leaves or long-tapering-clustered needles. Hemlock trees will have flattened, nearly two-ranked leaves, less than half an inch long; the undersides distinctly marked with two white lines. The white lines represent rows of sausage-shaped cells called guard cells. Microscopic stomas are tiny openings between the guard cells that allow the plant to release oxygen into the air and take carbon dioxide in. Life on this planet as we know it, depends on the functioning of these cells in every green plant on land and water.

Mature well-formed red spruce are handsome trees, developing a narrow, conical shape. The stiff, half-inch long, four-angled, evergreen needles appear to bristle around the stem in all directions. Birds associated with the conifers for food and cover include the golden-crowned kinglet, red-breasted nuthatch, Hermit thrush, black capped chickadee and tufted titmouse. Listen for the songs of these birds as you walk this trail. Blackwater Falls State Park has a naturalist on staff year round. If you wish to learn the birds by song and appearance, she is available to take park guests on guided walks.

Scotch pine is a native of the Scottish highlands and was introduced into this country as an ornamental. It has often been used for windbreaks, or shelterbelts to protect other vegetation. The foliage has a bluish-green cast to it and the tree grows with an open form producing a more rounded appearance at the ends of branches than the spruce or hemlock. The two-inch long needles occur in bundles of two; each needle appearing twisted and somewhat flattened.

Balsam fir is the only species of fir native to West Virginia. The spreading branches taper upward slightly forming a narrow, spire-like crown. The flattened, two-ranked evergreen needles may be up to an inch long. The strongly aromatic leaves are dark green above with two white bands beneath. Cup your hand around a branch and move it along the length of the twig to feel the pliable, waxy texture of the leaves and to release that spicy pine-like fragrance.

Some native understory species have migrated into this once brutally barren ground. As the trees have grown, periodically shedding their needles they have added to the meager soil substrate. Those plants, which you will find growing here, are naturally adapted to thin, acidic soils like the sphagnum moss and Lycopodium trailing across the ground.

The presence of bracken fern indicates a disturbed soil. Bracken fern looks rather coarse with its stout, dark-green foliage cut into three main segments. Each segment divides into many lace-like leaflets. Velvet-leaf blueberry which also invades disturbed soils, occurs in patches near the trail head and across the forest openings.

From the few historical accounts of the original forest conditions of Tucker County, it is known that hemlock-dominated stands occurred on the "tablelands" of the region. Parts of Blackwater Falls State Park would be included in this description. Look under the canopy and notice the large number of young hemlock seedlings. That is an indication that hemlock may become the dominant tree as the forest matures.

Species of trees found growing among the giant hemlocks include sugar maple, beech white ash, birch and wild black cherry—all species of trees occurring naturally on the greater portion of the trail further ahead. In fact, as the trail winds away from the lake to higher ground, the forest canopy changes to an open beech dominated woodland.

Beech trees hold their wispy, light brown leaves throughout the winter. On even slightly windy days, listen and you will hear them rattle in the wind, creating a somewhat dreamy, shadowy mood enhancing the solemn winter tones and deep silence. Scattered through the beech trees look for yellow birch, serviceberry, red maple, crab apple and mountain holly. In the summer months, observe the endless carpets of New York ferns spreading across the forest floor. Their pointed tips bend in all directions and forms even-waves in a breeze.

You may notice a near absence of oak. Oak trees are primarily associated with the forests at the lower elevations of the state, or in the canyon where there is deeper soil and more shelter from the ravaging winter winds. This explains why you will see fewer wild turkey in Blackwater State Park than you do in other parts of the state. Wild turkey depend heavily upon the acorns of oak trees in their diets.

The woods in the vicinity of this trail provides one of the best seats in West Virginia for close observation of two uncommon species of birds, the hermit thrush and the American woodcock. In the spring and summer, listen for the haunting song of the hermit thrush. The outward appearance of an adult male, with its brown back, spotted white breast and reddish tail gives no indication of the melodious notes it can produce. Look for an even drabber version of this species moving quietly about in the winter, for it is the only thrush that does not migrate southward for the winter.

The boggy ground under the forest canopy provides an ideal habitat for the woodcock as well. The male American woodcock displays quite an elaborate mating ritual every spring, usually in April at this high elevation. Starting at dusk, a male woodcock makes his way out of the woods to open ground and begins a spiraling upward-flight to well over 200 feet above the ground, hoping to win the love of a female woodcock. His stiffened outer feathers make a whistling sound as he ascends the night air. He begins a bubbly song as he hovers for a moment before descending quickly in a zig-zag pattern to the ground. Once on the ground, he utters a triumphant call of intermittent nasal "peents," and approaches his intended for an amorous conclusion to his mating dance. The woodcock display alone makes an early spring visit to Blackwater Falls State Park well worth the trip.

DOBBIN HOUSE TRAIL SYSTEM

The Dobbin House Loop Trail System has a difficulty rating of III. However, shorter sections are easier to walk. Marked with blue triangle blazes, the trail is about 2½ miles long, Pase Point Trail is a quarter mile long, one way. To access Dobbin House Trail, drive past the campground entrance and proceed toward Pendleton Lake. Just beyond the fork to Pendleton Point Overlook, you will see a nice wide trail off to the left. This old railroad bed will cross a large wooden bridge over Pendleton Run. Turn toward your left to follow the Dobbin House Trail. You will see the blue triangle blazes of the Allegheny Trail System that follows a section of Dobbin House Trail.

Proceed along this section of the trail for about three quarters of a mile to the junction with the Pase Point Trail. A half-mile walk beyond Dobbin House Trail will take you to a spectacular view of the canyon from a massive rock outcrop overlooking the union of the North Fork of the Blackwater River with the main channel. From late October through May, you can see the rail trail on the north wall of the canyon below you to the right.

Return to Dobbin House loop junction and turn left. The trail proceeds up through a stand of hardwoods to a reclaimed strip mine area. Proceed for about a mile to the junction of Woodcock Trail. Turn left to continue on Dobbin House Trail through a marshy area. The trail makes a sharp right turn to follow the boundary of the Monongahela National Forest and an extensive strip mine site for nearly three quarters of a mile. At the end of this section, the trail turns right in a steep descent through a wooded area above some beaver dams and then along Pendleton Lake back to the wooden bridge over Pendleton Run. **Bicycles permitted. Intermediate cross-country skiing. (See Dobbin House on Page 33)**

Across the first half- mile, the easy, gentle grade of Dobbin House Trail follows an old railroad grade along the canyon rim overlooking Pendleton Run. The trail turns away from Pendleton Run and follows the Blackwater River after about a quarter of a mile. There are several options for hiking within this trail system. Be sure to bring a light snack or a lunch and plenty of water if you intend to walk the loop—it is well worth it!

From late October through April, this section of Dobbin House Trail affords wide views of the Blackwater River Canyon. You can actually see the jumbled boulder fields on the stream bed some 400 to 500 feet below and observe precipitous rock outcrops on the opposite canyon wall. Once the foliage is on the trees during the growing season you must proceed to Pase Trail for views of the canyon.

Several interesting kinds of vegetation may be viewed year-round. Notice the lush stands of Lycopodium or club moss, carpeting the forest floor throughout the trail system. In the spring and early summer, the lovely Canada mayflower grows up between the dense carpet of Lycopodium. Spreading clumps of hay-scented and New York ferns grow in lush patches along the trail. Tall wands of interrupted fern and cinnamon fern grow sporadically throughout the area of this trail system. The forest along much of this stretch of the trail is fairly mature and very beautiful. In early July, expansive colonies of rhododendron are loaded with large whitish-pink blossoms.

Long, trailing vines of greenbrier or split-shins grow in dense patches over shrubs and up the trunks of trees along the first few hundred yards of the trail. In some places greenbrier stems extend out over the trail. Greenbrier reaches upward toward the sunlight with the aid of a pair of tendrils growing from the base of each leaf. These appendages wrap around the branches of other plants for support.

Look for the crisscrossing tracks of grouse in the snow cover along this trail. These birds seem to be fairly abundant on this side of the park. Also, I have seen a few signs of turkey in these woods. Due to the low amount of oak, turkey are not abundant at this elevation, but they are present.

Snowshoe hares have very sharp teeth that leave a clean, straight cut on the tips of plants they have fed on. Look for clean cuts on rhododendron and other shrubs about two feet off the ground for signs of their presence. The region around Blackwater Falls State Park has long been associated with this shy, northern species. You must look very closely for them in winter, as their white coats allow them to disappear against the background.

The most common tree species occurring along Dobbin House Trail are the same as in most other parts of Blackwater Falls State Park including black cherry, red maple, mountain holly, rhododendron, hemlock and yellow birch. Mountain laurel, smooth arrow-wood, and velvet leaf blueberry are the most common shrubs. However, just below the trail where the geology and soils begin to differ, the vegetation shifts to the central hardwoods. Below the trail, herbaceous plants increase in numbers and really flourish, and the number of species in the tree canopy increases as well.

Large leaves or fronds of the intermediate wood fern drape the sides of boulders and steep banks in this area. This is one of the few wood ferns to remain green all winter. Ruffled edges of intermediate wood fern may be seen peering out from under the winter snows.

Sporadically along the trail you will see stonewalls that were constructed when the Thompson's' built the first narrow gauge rail line from Davis to Douglas in the mid-1890's. The rail line skirted along this rim of the canyon to Douglas on the North Fork of the Blackwater River to transport timber cut from this area to the mill they built in Douglas.

The quarter-mile walk on to Pase Point Overlook from where Dobbin House Trail turns sharply away from the canyon is well worth the extra steps. From this side of the canyon, you will be captivated by the panoramic view of the canyon and the Blackwater Rail Trail just below the overlook on the north wall. The copiously photographed Lindy Run Overlook on the opposite canyon rim is also visible from the huge rock outcrop of Pase Point. Pase Point is named for a descendent of Jacob Pase, the man who first settled near Thomas, West Virginia.

Turkey vultures are a delightfully constant presence both in the air and on the rock outcrops. Often, in the early morning, a group of these graceful-flying ugly ducklings may be seen perched in a tree above the trail. They await the late-morning rising currents of warm air to take them aloft where they can better sniff out a meal.

It is quite a surprise to watch a kettle of vultures circle and land in the trees, or on the rocks. When sunbathing, they look statuesque with their massive wings outstretched and tiny heads held stiffly aloft.

The scientific name of the vulture family Cathartidae, is derived from the Greek word kathartes which means cleanser. Vultures serve as the unofficial sanitation police, in charge of the whole landscape. They are scavengers, feeding primarily on carrion. Their starkly bald red heads are nature's way of protecting the bird from disease, since it regularly plunges its head into the bowels of dead animals when feeding. Despite their table manners, few birds display such grace and power when soaring in wide sweeping circles. In the last decade or so, the increased population of crows may be competing with them somewhat.

After following the Pase Point Overlook Trail back to the Dobbin House juncture, turn left to walk up through a maturing stand of hardwood trees to the plateau. The first quarter-mile or so beyond the hardwoods, the trail begins an easy walk through an open spruce plantation. The area is a reclaimed strip mine. The dominant tree species is primarily red spruce, though some Norway spruce and hemlock were also planted.

Spattered with greenery, the shiny-black coal littered landscape effervesces a strange charm, like a moonscape struggling to resemble earth. A few Virginia pine and the very uncommon balsam poplar occur intermittently between young red spruce. Dense colonies of mountain laurel and rhododendron border the trail. To the left, look along the edges of the strip mine high wall you will see a tall grove of carefully planted Norway spruce gracing the ridge with their arching branches.

Mountain laurel is a colonial low-growing tree or shrub. Where soil is thin, highly acidic and dry, this plant just keeps on growing. Reaching an average height of six to ten feet, older colonies may grow to several meters in length due to the vegetative sprouting of new stems along the root system. Even branches of mountain laurel, which touch the ground, may initiate root growth and generate a new shoot.

The beautiful flowers produced by mountain laurel have beauty in their function as well as in their form. Five fused petals form a cup-like flower bearing two indentations in each petal. The whole flower is approximately one inch across. Ten sticky, red stamens arise from the center of the flower and bend towards the edge of the petals inserting the anthers in the depressions. One pistil erupts from the center of the flower.

Nectar-seeking insects like bumblebees land on the center of the flower, and as they probe for nectar may brush against one of the stamens. When this happens, the anther springs out of the depression towards the center showering the bee with its pollen. The bee will continue on its journey to another flower; where the pollen on its head may rub onto the pistil and pollinate that flower. If the flowering mechanism is ready, you may touch one of the stamens lightly to observe this springing mechanism for yourself.

This inter-dependent relationship between bumblebees and mountain laurel is only one of thousands of such intricate relationships between plants and animals. Without the seasonal unfolding of these events, the forest ecosystem would begin to break down. And even more amazing is how little we may still know about these kinds of inner workings in nature.

Two ponds are visible from the Dobbin House/Allegheny Trail where it intersects the Woodcock Trail. These ponds support a few plants and animals even though they are in the middle of an old strip mine. Common rush and glade St. Johnswort, upland willow and mountain laurel grow along or near the edges of the ponds.

Wood frogs and whirligig beetles live in the water. Dragon flies may be seen zooming across the water. Spring peepers have been found singing from reeds in the water.

Dwarf red spruce trees dot the black, sooty ground spreading their lower branches in a protective cover for birds and other wildlife. This relatively uninhabited location may provide a haven for the snowshoe hare. Decaying Lycopodium, lichens and dewberry add minute quantities of humus and color to bare rock. Life is struggling to reclaim this ground, and though slowly, it is winning. Despite the poor soil, several wild flowers grow under the laurel thickets including the lovely orchid called pink lady's slipper. Also during the growing season look for spotted wintergreen and Canada mayflower.

A short distance beyond the ponds, Dobbin House Trail turns sharply to the right where you can look across a wide plain of grass, rocks and scattered trees. This section of the trail goes in a straight line for nearly a mile along a boundary of the Monongahela National Forest and private property. Much of the private property to the left was a strip mine and has been reclaimed. Currently, there are active strip mines dominating the landscape on the lower end of the trail. On the right is a mature Norway spruce plantation.

Velvet leaf blueberry shrubs grow in dense

two-to-three foot high patches. The lovely reddish twigs look shiny due to the dense, short covering of fine hairs. Glade St. Johnswort is filling in some of the low wet places. And a fascinating grass called *beard grass* pops up in scattered locations along the trail. The top of this grass resembles a short, thick horses tail, or long beard.

The sharp contrast between the forest and disturbed land is startling, and thought provoking. In fact, maybe more trails need to provide this kind of contrast to remind us of the major impact that our culture is having on the land. Forest fragmentation, timbering, mall construction and highway development are gradually limiting the amount of untrammeled land where our natural, unseen life support system exists.

The coal that was removed from this land probably provided the electricity which kept us warm in the winter and provided the energy for the industries that made our boots, cameras, field glasses and—field guides. And though we have learned how to make pollution-free energy from the sun, we lack the political will to make the technological changes towards a more solar-based economy. Until we do, more beautiful places like Blackwater Falls State Park will sustain frayed and broken edges.

In the reclaimed strip mined land a few miles east of Dobbin House Trail, the bulldozers excavated a well-preserved fossilized track way. Scientists determined that the 300-million-year-old tracks were those of a rather large, extinct amphibian. This animal was alive before the dinosaurs had even evolved. The original fossil is maintained in the collection of the Carnegie Museum of Natural History in Pittsburgh, PA.

During the growing season, the Dobbin House Trail System supports an interesting array of song birds. Species commonly seen or heard includes the golden-crowned kinglet, purple finch, blackburnian warbler, field sparrow, swamp sparrow, solitary vireo, chipping sparrow, black-capped chickadee, woodcock and magnolia warbler. The ethereal sound of the hermit thrush trills through the trees at any time of day from mid-April through early July.

An Old Inn on the way to Fort Pendelton, Harper's New Monthly Magazine, *No. CCCLXII, July, 1880, Vol. LXI*

Pendleton Point Overlook

As the falls provide the scenic focal point on the south side of Blackwater Canyon, Pendleton Point Overlook draws equal attention

View of Pendleton Falls

on the north side. From the overlook at Pendleton Point, the view of Blackwater Canyon is impressive. This point

Pendleton Lake

allows you to look across the gaping canyon to Blackwater Lodge, or down the canyon for several miles. From mid-September to mid-October when the leaves on the hardwood trees have changed this place is absolutely stunning.

Beaver Lodge on Pendleton Lake

145

Animals Of The Park

If you discount the deer population on any given day, it would appear that very few animals live in Blackwater Falls State Park. But several species of common birds, mammals, reptiles and amphibians make a home in the sheltered nooks and crannies of the forest. As a result of the harsh environment, the number of species and total number of animals is somewhat less than you would find in an equal area of land with better soil and a more diverse mix of tree species. However, the extreme nature of the environment has created niches for several unusual kinds of animals.

REPTILES AND AMPHIBIANS:

The timber rattlesnake is one of the more unique species of the animal kingdom that inhabits the environs of Blackwater Falls State Park. It is a thick-bodied snake that attains a maximum length of about five feet long, rarely, six feet. The back-ground color on the snakes back may range from yellow to brown or black, with a series of dark

chevron-shaped bands across the back. The rattlesnake's rattle is one of those strange anomalies in nature. No other reptile, nor any other animal for that matter, has a structure similar to the rattle. The Timber Rattlesnake (Crotalus horridus) is a top predator in the forest ecosystems of eastern North America. It is found nowhere else in the world.

The rocky outcrops and ledges along the canyon rim provide an ideal habitat for rattlesnakes. They feed primarily on small mammals, and occasionally birds and bird eggs.

Frank Jernejcic, WV Wildlife Biologist-expert herpetologist, knows of two den sites within the vicinity of the Blackwater Canyon. He regularly leads a field trip to one of them during the West Virginia Nongame Wildlife event held at Blackwater Falls State Park every year. Other snakes which might be encountered in the park include the small northern-ringneck snake, the garter snake, northern water snake and the northern black racer.

A diverse population of salamanders flourish in the cool, damp environs of the canyon, including the threatened Cheat Mountain Salamander—see Page 96 under Elakala Trail. Only 28 species of salamanders are known to occur within West Virginia, and about half that number has been identified in Blackwater Falls

State Park. Species of greatest abundance include the mountain dusky salamander, Appalachian seal salamander, redback salamander, slimy salamander and Wehrle's salamander.

MAMMALS

A relatively small number of West Virginia's approximately 70 species of mammals are found in Blackwater Falls State Park. More unusual species inhabiting West Virginia may be seen in the park including snowshoe hare, black bear, fisher, bobcat, red squirrel and several unique species of warblers.

The rare and endangered Virginia northern flying squirrel is known to occur in a few areas near the canyon rim. The population in Blackwater Canyon is the southern most known population of this species. The squirrel does not actually fly, but with aid of loose skin along its sides is able to soar or glide from tree to tree. If you were to observe one of these animals, be sure and report it to the park naturalist whose office is located in Blackwater Lodge.

VIRGINIA NORTHERN FLYING SQUIRREL (*Glaucomys sabrinus fuscus*)
     <u>*General Description*</u>: Head and body about 5 ½ to 6 ½ inches long, with the tail nearly

as long as the body ranging from 4 ½ to 5 ½ inches long. The tail is more elongated and less bushy than the tail on the more common gray squirrel. Fur is shiny-looking, olive-brown above and white tipped on its belly. The ears are rounded and small.

Distinguishing Characteristic and Behaviors: The flying squirrel has folds of loose skin along the body from the front legs to the hind legs. When the squirrel jumps from a tree it spreads its arms out wide expanding the skin-flaps. The outstretched skin acts somewhat like a parachute, slowing the speed of descent and allowing the squirrel to safely glide across wide gaps between forest trees. Recent studies conducted by the WVDNR & US Forest Service have revealed an interesting fact about their feeding behavior. The work of wildlife biologist Donna Mitchell

has revealed that a major component of their diet is a group of fungi that form mycorrhizal associations with plants.

Mycorrhizal fungi aid spruce trees and other forest plants in obtaining essential nutrients and moisture for their growth. The Northern flying squirrel aids in dispersing the spores of the fungus through its droppings.

This important ecological relationship demonstrates another critical interdependence between a seemingly insignificant creature and the health and survival of a forest ecosystem.

Habitat: Prefers stands of large older trees in mixed hardwoods and red spruce forests. Has been found on the canyon rim and higher ridges above Blackwater Canyon. It is currently listed as federally endangered and found in only six counties of West Virginia.

SNOWSHOE HARE *(Lepus americanus)*

General Description: Rather large, ranging in length from 16 to 20 inches; height at shoulder about 8 inches; average weight is about 3 pounds. In the summer, its fur is grayish to brown, darker down its back and on its rump; whitish underneath on its abdomen and chin. In the winter, this hare is pure white with slightly darkish tipped ears. The change in the coat color is triggered by the number of hours of daylight.

Distinguishing characteristics: This animal is larger than the typical cottontail rabbit seen on farms fields, and weedy places in towns and has much longer ears. The long hind legs have large, hairy feet with long wide-spreading toes that form "snowshoes," allowing the animals to scamper across deep snows.

Habitat; Snowshoe hares are northern latitude animals and reach the southernmost extension of their range in West Virginia. They are limited to the spruce/hemlock woods where thick colonies of rhododendron provide good cover and food in winter. Their numbers are scarce, but might be seen where the rhododendron is thickest near the

Davis Trail , or Dobbin House Trail. If you see a pile of snipped rhododendron leaves under a rhododendron, then you have seen a place where the snowshoe hare has been feeding. They will bite off the leaves, in order to feed on the twigs.

Behavior: Snowshoe hares will eat berries, spruce buds, twigs and bark. They are shy, secretive animals of the deep forest and normally not seen out in the open making them difficult to observe. These animals are very fast runners. They have been clocked at speeds as high as 30 m.p.h. They tend to make their home in a depression in the leaf litter on a knoll well above the wet boggy ground associated with the spruce woods.

BEAVER *(Castor canadensis)*

General Description: A beaver is essentially, a big rodent. Rodents are animals that gnaw with their front teeth. Average length is about 45 inches. A fourth of the animal's length is in the flat, hairless tail, which averages ten inches long and nearly five inches wide. When dry, an adult beaver is a dark reddish-brown color above, with lighter under parts. When they are wet, beaver appear quite sleek and black in color. A three year-old-adult will weigh between 45 and 50 pounds on the average.

Distinguishing characteristics: The beaver's tail is the primary characteristic distinguishing it from a muskrat. Also, the head has a more triangular shape to it; this is quite evident when they are seen swimming in the water with just the head on the surface. The prominent four front teeth look orange—if you can get close enough to see them.

Habitat: Beaver used to be found all over the United States before they were nearly hunted to extinction for their pelts. They were extirpated in West Virginia by 1825, and reintroduced in 1933 from populations in Michigan and Wisconsin into the mountain counties of West Virginia. Beaver will be found where there are streams, lakes, ponds and trees. One of the major activities of beaver is the damming of streams to create water deep enough for them to conceal a lodge or burrow entrance. Beaver are prevalent throughout the Blackwater drainage basin. There is an old abandoned lodge located on the shore just above the swimming area of Pendleton Lake. Numerous beaver dams are located on Pendleton Run just outside the park boundary. They can be viewed by climbing the steps up to the Western Maryland Railroad grade at the upper end of Pendleton Lake.

Behavior: Beaver have a complex set of behaviors and activities all relative to the environmental conditions around them.

When beaver first move into an area, the first thing they will do is look for a site to construct a dam. Some scientists believe that the sound of running water triggers this instinctive behavior. They will stop construction when they no longer hear running water. A dam is built by first embedding sticks into the bottom of the stream parallel to the flow of water. They then place mud on top of the sticks. They will alternate these layers of sticks, mud and rocks until they have a pond of a satisfactory depth.

Beaver like to feed on the bark of many species of deciduous trees but they have definite preferences. Beaver will eat the trees close to their dam site first and then work a few hundred yards away from the pond. They fell a tree by carefully gnawing around the base and can determine where and when the tree will fall. A tree will then be cut into sizes small enough to lug to the pond to store for winter use.

Their favorite species of the northern hardwoods forest includes serviceberry, aspen, willow, black cherry, yellow birch, black birch, witch hazel, alder, red maple and beech. Based on this list you can see that they would be well fed in Blackwater Falls State Park. In the summer, they eat lots of herbaceous plants including sedges, cattails, blackberry leaves and goldenrod.

BLACKBEAR (*Euarctos americanus*)

General Description: Black bears are usually black in color, or rusty-black with long, soft fur. They are considered to be a medium-sized bear averaging about 4 ½ to 6 ½ feet in length. Shoulder height may range from 30 to 40 inches. The average black bear in this area will weigh between 200 and 300 pounds. An unusually large male may weigh as much as 500 pounds. Females are usually smaller than males. Front claws are fairly short and curved. The snout is fairly long and somewhat pointed.

Distinguishing Characteristics: Only bear in West Virginia. If you see a bear that looks nothing like the description above, climb the nearest and tallest tree you can find.

Habitat: Black bears live in deciduous woods. They have very large territories where they spend a good part of their time wandering in search of food. Males have much larger territories than females, whose primary concern is maintaining a habitat large enough to provide food and shelter for herself and her cubs.

Behavior: Bears are omnivorous, eating berries, roots, leaves, small mammals, insects and even small fawns if they are lucky enough to find and overtake one. Bears spend most of their day foraging for food. They are intelligent and curious, and though they have a natural fear of people, they will sometimes trespass into areas inhabited by people. They may be lured by the smell of garbage or cooking food. **BEARS SHOULD NEVER BE FED**, and always discouraged away

from areas used by people. If they are allowed to become familiar with people, they can become a danger.

WOODLAND JUMPING MOUSE
(Napaeozapus insignis)

    General Description: Brownish-yellow mouse with long, coarse hair and a white belly; body 3 3/5 to- 4 inches long; tail 5 to 6 inches.

    Distinguishing Characteristics: Sides are bright yellow and this mouse has large hind feet. The long tail is white tipped. Generally weighs less than an ounce. The animal has small ears and short front legs.

    Habitat: Forested areas or open fields, look particularly near the bogs and glades around the campground.

    Behavior: This little critter can jump from  10 to 12 feet in a single leap; however, average jump distance is more like 4 to 7 feet. Will eat up to half its body weight in grass seeds, flower heads of daisies or young spruce needles during the summer. May occasionally eat insects and spiders. Look for piles of grass stems cut into 4-inch pieces.

FISHER *(Martes pennanti)*

The fisher (once called "Black Cat of the Spruces") was once a predominant predator of the spruce forests and high mountain regions of West Virginia. The last one was killed near the Coal River in 1863. They were hunted for their pelts and for the fact that they were considered to be a threat to livestock. Re-introduced to West Virginia in the 1960's, twenty-five young fisher were brought to the state from New Hampshire in exchange for wild turkey. Fifteen of those animals were released into Tucker County.

General Description: The head and body may range from 20 to 25 inches in length; the tail adds another 10 to 13 inches.

Distinguishing characteristics: The fur ranges from dark-brown to black, with white specks at the tips of the hairs over most of the body; body is slim and the tail rather busy.

Habitat; where to look for them: May be seen anywhere in the park. However, they are scarce in the area.

Behavior: Fisher feed primarily on small mammals, birds and even carrion. They may be

active during the day as well as the night. They build their dens in hollow trees or in the ground.

WHITETAIL DEER *(Odocoileus virginianus)*

CAUTION! DEER MAY BE HARMFUL TO OVERALL FOREST HEALTH. Deer are more than abundant in Blackwater Falls State Park, notice the lack of brush throughout the woods. Many wildlife biologists and forest ecologists are certain the number of deer are having a severely negative impact on the tree seedlings, shrub cover and wildflowers. The small, scrawny size of individual deer is probably due to a lack of adequate nutrition and in-breeding in the deer herd. Enjoy them from a safe distance however, **DO NOT FEED THEM! Ask your park naturalist for a brochure explaining in detail why deer and other wildlife should not be fed.**

General Description: Whitetail deer stand about three to four feet high at the shoulder. They have light-brown fur with slightly lighter shades underneath.

Distinguishing characteristics: The fur takes on a slight reddish cast in the summer, and the underside of the tail is white.

Habitat: Whitetail deer are a forest species, however, they have taken advantage of the abundant food source in the fields and forest edge habitat created by people.

Behavior: Whitetail deer spend much of their day browsing the forest foliage for food. They eat twigs of shrubs and trees, fruits, grasses and other herbaceous plant life. When food is scarce, they browse the leaves and twigs of rhododendron, mountain laurel and seedlings of trees on the forest floor. Deer are normally shy animals and run once the presence of people is detected. However, in parks where they are protected their behavior is markedly different. Deer have become a menace in some places, where they will wander close by roads and trails to beg for food.

RED SQUIRREL (common name—spruce squirrel) (*Tamiasciurus hudsonicus*)

General Description: The head and the body of this active little mammal is about 7 to 8 inches long. Its tail may be as long as 6 inches though 4 or 5 is the average. Its fur has a uniformly reddish color.

Distinguishing characteristics: In the summer this animal has a faint black line along  its sides and a distinct white belly. In winter it has ear tufts, and the fur color is not as distinct between the top and underparts.

Habitat: This animal prefers to live in spruce or other conifer woods, or mixed hardwoods and conifers. Red squirrels are commonly seen and heard throughout the park.

Behavior: Quite active during the day feeding on conifer seeds, nuts, eggs and even fungi. Red squirrels will store the cones of conifers for later use. Look for little tips of red spruce stems along the trails. Red squirrels will nip these off of the trees when feeding. Call is a noisy ratchet-like sound, heard frequently during the day from the limbs of spruce high above the forest floor.

LONGTAIL WEASEL (*Mustela frunata*)

General Description: Average body length is between 8 and 10 inches. Weasels are long, sleek mammals. Fur is dark reddish brown.

Distinguishing characteristics: The head is slightly larger than its neck; it has a black tip on its tail, and yellowish-white underparts.

Habitat: Found throughout forested and open glade-like areas, but prefers to be near water. Longtail weasels may be seen most anywhere in the park.

Behavior: Longtail weasels feed primarily on small mammals but will also take birds and other small animals. They are active both night and day roaming the ground in search of food; may also climb trees when hunting. Weasels kill their prey by piercing the back of the skull with their very sharp canine teeth.

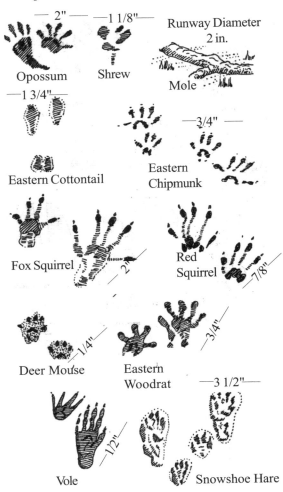

— 2" —
Opossum

— 1 1/8" —
Shrew

Runway Diameter
2 in.
Mole

—1 3/4"—
Eastern Cottontail

—3/4"—
Eastern Chipmunk

Fox Squirrel
— 2"

Red Squirrel
— 7/8"

Deer Mouse
1/4"

Eastern Woodrat
3/4"

Vole
1/2"

— 3 1/2" —
Snowshoe Hare

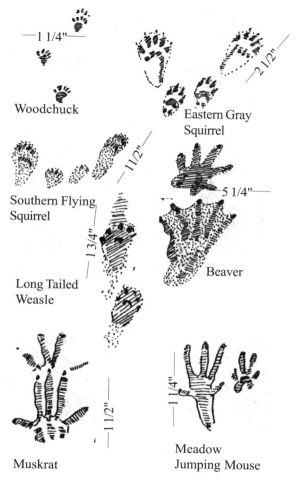

—1 1/4"—

Woodchuck

2 1/2"

Eastern Gray
Squirrel

Southern Flying
Squirrel

1 1/2"

5 1/4"

1 3/4"

Long Tailed
Weasle

Beaver

Muskrat

1 1/2"

1 1/4"

Meadow
Jumping Mouse

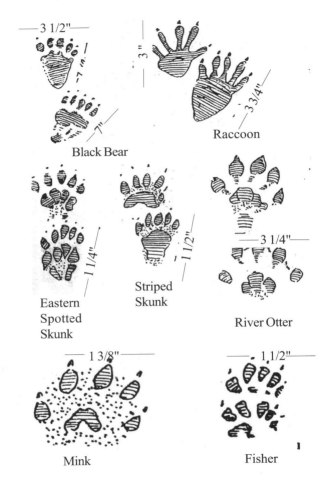

3 1/2"

Black Bear

3"

3 3/4"

Raccoon

Eastern Spotted Skunk

1 1/4"

Striped Skunk

1 1/2"

River Otter

3 1/4"

Mink

1 3/8"

Fisher

1 1/2"

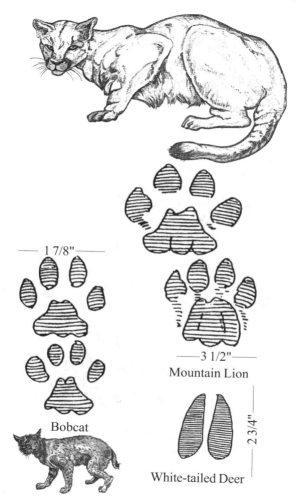

1 7/8"

Bobcat

3 1/2"

Mountain Lion

2 3/4"

White-tailed Deer

BIRDS

The bird life of Blackwater Falls State Park is one of the main wildlife attractions. Just like the vegetation, the songbirds include species associated with the northern boreal forests of Canada. Several of these unique bird species are year-round residents, though most are included in the group known as neo-tropical migrants.

Neo-tropical migrants are species that actually live in Central or South America but come north into the United States during the summer months to breed. Sadly, scientists have noticed a definite decline in the numbers of these birds over the past twenty or thirty years. The loss of rain forest habitat coupled with the habitat destruction and fragmentation in the United States has been identified as contributing to the declining numbers.

One thing that may help in the United States and especially in West Virginia is the creation of unbroken tracts of forest along the spine of the Appalachian Mountains (Allegheny Mountains here), and along the river corridors. Another problem contributing to their decline may be the rapacious feeding of too many deer, reducing the cover and food source for these birds.

Though many of the beautiful bird species which occur in the park are fewer in numbers than they once were, they still return each spring to brighten the woods with wondrous melodies. The major groups you will see and hear includes the thrushes, warblers, vireos, sparrows and species having only one or two representatives of their genus or family in the park.

The most predominant attribute of Blackwater Falls State Park in the winter, besides the snow, is the silence. Though some beautiful birds, big and small are found here in winter, they are for the most part low in numbers and rather elusive. Look for birds around the buildings and open glades near Pendleton Lake in winter. Brown creepers, winter wrens and red-breasted nuthatches are fairly common in the woods but you have to pay close attention to see them.

Black capped chickadees and juncos are fairly common throughout the more open areas of the park in winter. Also look for tufted titmouse.

The most brightly colored birds of summer, with delightful songs are usually difficult to see. The male birds perch high in the canopy to declare their territory when singing. You will hear most birds before you see them. The female birds are usually drab and are either sitting on the nest or quietly foraging for food. Actually seeing many of the birds described below takes a lot of patience and time.

Following are individual descriptions of a few selected representatives of the more unique birds. The **appearance describes the males only.** Females are usually less brightly colored and less visible. If you are serious about birds, you will already have or at least want to acquire a general field guide. The characteristics of female birds are described in most field guides.

TURKEY VULTURE *(Cathartes aura)*

Appearance: Length, 26" to 32 "; wing span 68" to 72"; bare skin of head and neck red; feathers dark on upper body; outer wing feathers along the under surface is whitish-gray; turkey vultures have prominent eyes, a short neck which can be pulled down into a tuft of feathers at base of the neck

Behavior: Turkey vultures are graceful in flight. They will soar effortlessly to great heights during the day on waves of warm air currents rising from the canyon floor. In flight, the wings are held in a "V" shaped manner. They spend their time in the air

searching for carrion (dead animals). They can spot a dead animal as small as a mouse from as far away as 300 feet. Look for them sitting on tree tops with outstretched wings, sunning themselves on sunny days.

Habitat: They often roost on cliffs or trees in groups. Roosting vultures are often seen from Dobbin House Trail on the rock outcrops jutting out over the canyon. Turkey vultures are one of the most visible animals in the park making regular sweeps overhead, swaying in the breeze as they relentlessly scan the ground and sniff the air for a meal.

WINTERWREN *(Troglodytes troglodytes)*

Appearance: Length, no more than 3 ½ inches; plump, chestnut-brown bird with stubby tail held erect.

Behavior: The most beautiful song in the Appalachian forests; song is a long series of sweet-trilling notes; it mimics the joy of splashing water and all things eternal; it creeps about the moss covered logs and rocks on forest floor looking for insects; builds a nest in a cavity on the ground, well concealed in a fissure of rock, under a log or in a rotten stump.

Habitat: Prefers conifers during nesting season, spruce or hemlock; will spend winters in thickets in ravines of hardwoods as well as conifer stands. Elakala Trail, Cherry Lane Trail, Dobbin House Trail and other areas of park.

DARK-EYED JUNCO *(Junco hyemalis)*

Appearance: Length about 5 ¼ inches long; head, back and throat uniformly gray; white on outer tail feathers that flash when bird flies; white bill and whitish belly.

Behavior: Song is a musical, rapid precession of high-pitched notes which stay about the same pitch, song ends with a clicking sound;

Perky little bird, hops on ground searching for insects and seeds; summer diet primarily insects and winter diet primarily seeds; builds nest on the ground in concealed location

Habitat: Prefers edges of mixed coniferous/deciduous woods. Especially visible near lodge, glades around Pendleton Lake; seen year-round.

BROWN CREEPER *(Certhia familiaris)*

Appearance: Length 4 ¾ inches; slim built bird with heavily streaked brown back, white below - well camouflaged against bark of trees; long tapering tail and long, thin curved bill.

Behavior: Song is a short series of very high-pitched notes; Moves in a slow spiral motion around the trunks of trees working from the base to the top foraging for insects; uses long stiff tail to brace itself while feeding and crawling around tree; will fly from top of one tree to the base of the next to begin feeding again; secretive bird; builds nest under flaps of loose bark on dead or dying trees.

Habitat: Prefers mature deciduous or conifer forest with large trees; common in the park in the winter and less common in the summer. Cherry Lane Trail, Yellow Birch Trail, Shay Trail and Elakala Trail good places to look.

PURPLE FINCH *(Carpodacus purpureus)*

Appearance: Length 5½ inches; raspberry colored sparrow-like bird; color concentrated around head, down the back and chest; dark eyes.

Behavior: Song is a fast, sweet warble with a distinct tweaking chip given at the end or in flight; searches for insects and seeds up in trees and shrubs, or in low brush near the ground; eats seeds, buds and berries; builds nest on horizontal branch of conifer tree at least 20 feet above the ground.

Habitat: Prefers edges of coniferous woodlands during breeding season; common year round near lodge, and in summer at snack-bar near Blackwater Falls.

WOODCOCK *(Philohela minor)*

Appearance: Length about 8 ½ inches long; stocky, rotund inland sandpiper with a short neck and short legs, and a long pointed bill; overall brown plumage with dark mottling makes this bird well camouflaged against dead leaves on the ground; has short-rounded wings and broad bars on head.

Behavior: Call is a series of short bleats made from the ground to attract female during nesting season; elaborate flight ritual involves whistling sounds made from air passing through tips of feathers as bird descends after upward spiral flight; feeds mainly on earthworms and insect larvae in ground; tip of bill is very sensitive and will detect any moving insects.

Habitat: Prefers wet meadows, shrub swamps or moist woods; ideal habitat is a mix of woods and open fields; spends the night protected in the forest and the day feeding in open areas. They are especially common in the mixed woods and fields around Pendleton Lake.

VEERY *(Hylocichla fuscescens)*

Appearance: Length about 6 inches; brownish cast on upper parts with a few brown spots on throat; whitish belly; faint, dull white eye ring.

Behavior: Song is a beautiful, breezy, series of flute-like notes tumbling down a musical scale; call note at end a brusque "phew"; nests on the ground in dense undergrowth; eats mostly

Veery

berries and insects; forages by hopping on the ground or through low vegetation looking for insects.

Habitat: Damp deciduous woods; prefers heavy understory. Listen for the song of the veery rising up from the canyon at any of the overlooks in the park; especially at dusk when the sun is setting, there is simply no other sound more hauntingly peaceful than the song of the veery.

HERMIT THRUSH *(Hylocichla guttata)*

Appearance: Length about 6 inches; brown back with heavily spotted white breast and rufous tail.

Behavior: Song is a melancholy, flute-like set of 3 or 4 phrases at different pitches; eerily beautiful; forages on the ground in search of insects and berries; slowly flicks tail when perched; nest built on the ground in well concealed area.

Habitat: Mixed damp, coniferous and deciduous woods; prefers a heavy understory. Listen for the song of the hermit thrush at the Pendleton Lake and in the woods along most of the trails. This bird is very common throughout the park.

BIRD LIST OF FREQUENTLY SEEN SPECIES

m= migrant; su=summer resident;
p= permanent resident

Great blue heron—m
Turkey vulture—p
Black vulture—p
Canada goose—m
Mallard—m
Cooper's hawk—su
Broad-winged hawk—su
Ruffed grouse—p
Sharp-shinned hawk—su
Wild turkey—p
Killdeer—p
Spotted sandpiper—m
Solitary sandpiper—m
American woodcock—su
Screech owl-p
Barred owl- p
Belted kingfisher—p
Northern flicker—p
Hairy woodpecker—p
Downy woodpeckor—p
Yellow-bellied
        sapsucker—m
Great crested
        flycatcher—su
Alder flycatcher—su
Solitary vireo—su
Red-eyed vireo—su
Blue jay—p
American crow—p
Common raven—p

Black-capped
        chickadee—p
Tufted titmouse—p
Brown creeper—p
White-breasted
        nuthatch—p
Red-breasted nuthatch—p
Carolina wren—p
Winter wren—p
Golden-crowned
        kinglet—p
Veery—su
Hermit thrush—su
Wood thrush—su
American robin—su
Cedar waxwing—p
Northern parula—su
Common yellow-
        throat—su
Ovenbird—su
Louisiana waterthrush—su
Magnolia warbler—su
Blackburnian warbler—su
Yellow-rumped
        warbler—su
Canada warbler—su
Field sparrow—p
Swamp sparrow—su
Chipping sparrow—su
Purple finch—su

Common Trees Of Blackwater Falls State Park

In tandem with bare rocks, trees are the primary natural elements visibly characterizing Blackwater Falls State Park. A small number of tree species compete with one another for dominance over limited resources. One of the more distinctive characteristics of both plant and animal communities in this park is the limited diversity. You will see the following species of trees on most every trail in the park.

YELLOW BIRCH
(Betula alleghaniensis)

EASTERN HEMLOCK
(Tsuga canadensis)

RED SPRUCE
(Picea rubens)

AMERICAN BEECH
(Fagus grandifolia)

WILD BLACK CHERRY
(Prunius serotina)

BIG TOOTH ASPEN
(Populus grandidentata)

RED MAPLE
(Acer rubrum)

STRIPED MAPLE
(Acer pennsylvanicum)

TULIP POPLAR
(Liriodendron tulipifera)

SMOOTH SERVICEBERRY
(Amelanchier laevis)
Juneberry and
COMMON SERVICEBERRY
(Amelanchier arborea.) "Sarvice"

MOUNTAIN HOLLY
(Ilex montana)

Additional Trees Found In
Blackwater Falls State Park

HARDWOODS

BLACK BIRCH
AMERICAN BASSWOOD
WHITE ASH
COMMON CHOKECHERRY
RED ELDERBERRY
AMERICAN ELM
BLACK GUM
HACKBERRY
SUGAR MAPLE
NORTHERN RED OAK
WHITE OAK
SASSAFRAS
SOURWOOD
SYCAMORE
MOUNTAIN MAGNOLIA

CONIFERS

SCOTCH PINE
NORWAY SPRUCE
VIRGINIA PINE
WHITE PINE
BALSAM FIR

Selected Shrubs Wild-flowers, and Non-Vascular Plants

Selected Shrubs Wildflowers, and Non-Vascular Plants

COMMON CLUBMOSS

TREE CLUBMOSS

GROUNDPINE

STIFF CLUBMOSS

POLYTRICHUM MOSS

SPHAGNUM MOSS

GRASSES AND SEDGES

COTTONGRASS

CAREX STRICTA

CAREX CRINITA

CAREX FOLLICULATA

SMALL
BURREED

COMMON
RUSH

SWEET
VERNAL GRASS

WILDFLOWERS AND FERNS

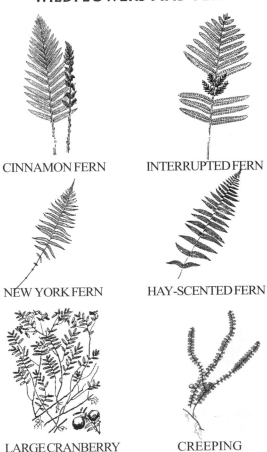

CINNAMON FERN

INTERRUPTED FERN

NEW YORK FERN

HAY-SCENTED FERN

LARGE CRANBERRY

CREEPING
SNOWBERRY

TEABERRY

PARTRIDGEBERRY

BOG GOLDENROD

SUNDEW

CANADA
MAYFLOWER

ORANGE
HAWKWEED

COMMON SHRUBS

BROOKSIDE ALDER

SPECKLED ALDER

**VELVETLEAF
BLUEBERRY**

WITCH HAZEL

**GLADE
ST. JOHNS WORT**

MOUNTAIN LAUREL

RHODODENDRON

**HERCULES' CLUB, OR
DEVIL'S WALKING
STICK**

DEWBERRY

MOUNTAINASH

WILD RAISIN

COMMON GREENBRIER

Plant List

PLANT LIST

Common Plant Names of Vascular Plants
According to *Flora of West Virginia*.
See Bibliography.

Non-Vascular Plants

bog clubmoss
marginal shield fern
interrupted fern
carpet moss
tree clubmoss
Christmas fern
bracken fern
groundpine
hair-cap moss or Polytrichum
stiff clubmoss

cinnamon fern
common clubmoss
intermediate wood
    fern
sensitive fern
slender clubmoss
sphagnum moss
hay-scented fern

New York fern

Vascular plants

broad-leaved cattail
watershield
woolgrass
heal-all
wood nettle
Carex stricta
soapwort
common chickweed
Carex folliculata
turtlehead
round-leaved sundew

common greenbrier

ladies tresses
cotttongrass
narrowleaf gentian
lamb's quarters
Carex crinita
spreading dogbane
creeping buttercup
small burreed
common plantain

frog hair
Quaker ladies (bluets)
common cinquefoil
common rush
Joe Pye weed
white wood sorrel
Canada mayflower
cardinal flower
tasselrue
painted trillium
dandelion
teaberry
Indian cucumber-root
field pussytoes
sweet white violet
carrion flower
orange hawkweed
common blue violet
beechdrops
common evening primrose
downy rattlesnake plantain
Appalachian blue violet

Virginia strawberry
Eleocharis
sneezeweed
dewberry
beak rush
cut-leaf coneflower
jewelweed
wild yam
bog goldenrod
wood anemone
white clintonia
coltsfoot
partridgeberry
pink lady's slipper
mouse-ear hawkweed
downy yellow violet
Turk's cap lily
English daisy
large cranberry
creeping snowberry

Surrounding Attractions and Trails

You may contact the Park Naturalist at Blackwater Falls State Park for information concerning any of the surrounding attractions.

BLACKWATER CANYON RAIL TRAIL

Approx. 14-miles long one way. Trail may be accessed in Thomas, WV, at the juncture of Rt. 32 and 27; or from Hendricks, Rt. 73; or along the Dry Fork River at the edge of Parsons. Parking is available but limited at each of these locations. The distance from Thomas to Hendricks is about 10 miles, from Hendricks, it is about four miles on to Parsons. Contact the US Forest Service for a map and more information at the Monongahela National Forest Supervisor's Office, 200 Sycamore Street, Elkins, 26241 or phone 304/636-1800.

Blackwater River Rail Trail

Though not accessible from Blackwater Falls State Park, this well maintained Rail Trail, visible from Pace Point Overlook, will allow you to truly experience the grandeur of this remarkable land, and allow you to traverse through a significant portion of the industrial history described in the first chapter.

Blackwater Canyon Rail Trail follows a 14-mile section of the old Western Maryland Railroad. The trail is included in the section of the Western Maryland Railroad built by Henry Gassaway Davis from Piedmont, Maryland, through Thomas to Elkins. The tracks were completed through Parsons in 1890. Trains continued to clamber up and down the canyon until 1984.

For the first two miles, you will walk past sleepy little communities nestled against green hillsides. These places were once-thriving industrial towns. Beginning along the banks of the North Fork of the Blackwater River in the still populated town of Thomas, the trail winds past reclaimed steep-walled strip mines and rows of beehive coke ovens, partially reclaimed by trees and wildflowers.

The North Fork River surges on with buoyant exhilaration over rocks stained orange from years of acid mine drainage that left the stream

Beehive Coke Ovens

devoid of life for many years. It is unbelievable to think that this is the very location so eloquently described by Philip Pendleton Kennedy in the Blackwater Chronicle. Funneling the stream over a limestone bed is currently treating the water. This brings the pH of the water to a level that allows the river to support aquatic insects and trout.

Below the coke ovens at Douglas, look for a cranberry bog on the right side of the trail. Sphagnum moss and cinnamon fern add beauty to this low wet ground. A hundred or more species of trees and herbaceous plants grow in profusion along this section of the trail.

Lying beside the trail just before it slips into the huge forests of the canyon is a large, solid-steel safe—a remnant from the industrial boom days at the turn of the century. This rusted vault, lying belly-up, with its legs angled up toward the sky has flowers growing from its large interior. It seems like a metaphor for the demise of the industrial past, which left the land and people with very little, but hope for more prosperous times.

Cinnamon fern growing on polytrichum moss hummocks in bog/glades near campground.

The trail passes between the first of many rock outcrops visible over the next six miles, at the end of the fields. Large colonies of rhododendron peer over the rocks. Hemlock trees line the hillside as the North Fork begins its plunge to join the main stem of the Blackwater River.

By the time you have reached the confluence of the North Fork and the Blackwater, you will be at least 300 feet in elevation above the water. Hardwood trees including

Abandoned safe along Blackwater River Rail Trail

tulip poplar, sugar maple, black cherry, and red maple tower above and below the trail from this point on.

The trail passes huge rock outcrops and slide areas over the next mile. One bank, which exposes a shale outcrop, may yield a few fern fossils from the Pennsylvanian age rock strata. Piles of railroad ties, and old telegraph poles are common throughout the length of the trail from this point on.

About two miles into the canyon, the forest becomes spectacular and remains so until you reach Hendricks. Large, widely spaced trees, their straight trunks rising a hundred feet or more, extend in a seemingly endless parade to the bottom and top of the canyon. Many wildflowers grow in abundance between the trees and scattered boulders.

Lush, dense patches of ramps occur throughout this rich forest. Spring wildflowers beginning at the end of April spread across the hillsides. Species to look for include foam flower, large-flowered trillium, toothwort, wild ginger, marsh blue violet, sweet white violet, common blue violet, dwarf ginseng, blue cohosh, black cohosh, Virginia waterleaf and many more.

Two large tributaries of the North Fork called Tub Run and Big Run will compel you to stop and gaze at the splashing water, rushing over massive rock cliffs and jumbles of giant boulders. Fed by cool water and protected by shade, the sides of these hollows are excellent places to look for spring wildflowers.

The music of the river hundreds of feet below rises constantly, filling the canyon with a soft rhythmic sound to accompany your journey. The wide riverbed is sometimes visible, especially in the spring before the leaf canopy is full. Other music you will hear spring through fall includes the songs of the winter wren, black-throated-green warbler, black-throated-blue warbler, parula warbler, solitary vireo, red-eye vireo, veery and many more.

Wildlife is abundant, but not regularly seen since most animals are camouflaged, move quietly, and many species are nocturnal. Black bear, red squirrels, chipmunks, least weasel, longtail weasel, grouse, turkey, deer mouse, red spotted newt, black rat snake, box turtle, and rattlesnakes have been seen. Many other species of small mammals, salamanders and reptiles are abundant, but seen even less often. The rare northern water shrew (*Sorex palustris punctulatis)* lives and feeds in the cold-water streams of the canyon. It patters through the water with its tiny webbed-feet and waterproof coat in search of aquatic insects.

At the bottom of the canyon the trail follows along the banks of the river for a mile or more before crossing through the town of Hendricks. A large limestone rock outcrop is visible on the right side of the trail. The expanse of limestone found along the lower end of the Blackwater River and along the Dry Fork naturally neutralizes the acidity of the streams.

Thomas, Coketon and Douglas

Along the Blackwater River Rail Trail, you will pass through Thomas, and the ghost towns of Coketon and Douglas. These three towns evolved around the mining industry. The charming tourist town of Thomas started as the center of the Davis Coal and Coke Company operation. The first settler near Thomas was a farmer named Jacob Pase, who settled on a hill above the town in 1880.

Henry Gassaway Davis opened his first coal mine near Thomas in 1883, just before the railroad was completed to the town. The city grew rapidly over the next 2 to 5 years as immigrants migrated with their families to settle in the town and work in the mines. By 1892, the community was incorporated as a town, with a population of nearly 700 people.

In 1901, the town was nearly destroyed by a huge fire. But within two years, nearly 100 new buildings were rebuilt including the Cottrill Opera House that is still standing, and has currently been renovated. A series of plays are open to the public in the summer. The town is tightly packed in layers on a steep hill above the North Fork of the Blackwater River. The buildings facing front street, all date back to the turn of the century. A nice tourist industry is growing where many of these old buildings have been renovated into bookstores, craft stores and restaurants.

The compact row of newly decorated buildings facing the tranquil North Fork of the Blackwater River are visited by tourists who are primarily passing through to other destinations. We, the modern tourists cannot fathom the sights, sounds and smells of everyday life that filled the streets and buildings just 80 years ago. The life-blood of the town was the coal and coke business. Hundreds of immigrant families moved to Thomas from Italy, Germany, Slovenia and other European Countries to work in the mines.

Imagine hearing three or four different languages spoken amid the hub of voices, train whistles and factory sounds. Many of the folks were dressed in European clothing until they became fully acclimated to life in the United States, or had earned enough money to buy more conventional styles. First names like Vincenzo,

Antonio, Vincent and Dandra were as common as John, Joe or Frank. The lives of children were quite different then also. Boys as young as 14 went to work in the mines, and some died in the mines before reaching adulthood.

Mining was very dangerous work in those early years. It still is, but was more so then before regulations were imposed on mining companies. The Davis Coal and Coke Company made efforts to keep the mines safe. For example, ventilation equipment was set up in the mines to alleviate the problem of deadly gases known to accumulate in underground mines.

However, on a Monday morning, February 4, 1907, the systems failed and a terrible mining accident occurred in Mine number 25 just outside of Thomas. The fans, which were supposed to

Buxton & Landstreet Department Store

keep fresh air circulating through the mine, had been out of commission over the weekend. Just as 25 men were entering the mine at 6:30 AM, a spark from a lamp, or cigarette (no none knows for certain) caused a terrible explosion killing all 25 people, including a 15-year-old boy named Oscar Allen.

Of the 25 killed, 16 had their deaths recorded. The names of the other nine men, recently immigrated, were not listed because no one knew them yet. These men are all buried in the Catholic cemetery in Thomas. Many of the victims had no families or friends and their graves are not marked. If you go to the cemetery, you will see a long row of unmarked graves where their bodies were laid side-by-side.

Coketon was a small suburb just south of Thomas. The rail trail goes through this area, or you can drive to it by taking route 27 which cuts to the right off of Route 32 as you are leaving town. The Davis Coal and Coke company

*Davis Coal
& Coke
Building*

building and the once famous Buxton and Landstreet Department Store are located about ½ mile below Thomas. These buildings are worth seeing for they are all that remain of the once boisterous industrial communities.

Also, ½ mile below these buildings look for the rows of beehive coke ovens. Inside, you will see the brick on the ceiling melted like glass from the intense heat that was once produced inside the ovens. Growing between the jumble of brick on the floors of the ovens are sweet, colorful ferns and wildflowers. According to several historical accounts, there were 1000 ovens in operation at the peak of the coke industry from 1890 to 1930. At night, the glow from the coke ovens could be seen for miles.

Douglas, located 1½ miles below Thomas, was a small town that built up around several coal mines opened by H.G. Davis. The town died in the 1930's with the demise of the coke industry and closing of the mines. Just a few of the 45 or so houses still remain in this once busy town. The beautiful 30-foot waterfall on the North Fork of the Blackwater River at Douglas is the site so vividly described by Phillip Pendleton Kennedy in the *Blackwater Chronicle*.

Canaan Loop Road

The Canaan Loop Road (CLR) has been referred to earlier in the discussion on the history of the region. This road makes an 18-mile loop from Davis through Blackwater Falls State Park, across Canaan Mountain and back to Davis and the park by way of Route 32. Most of this road traverses through the Monongahela National Forest and is also identified as Forest Road (FR) 13 on Forest Service maps. Many sections of it follow the old railroad grades, which led to and from the Davis sawmills.

The road is shaped like a very flattened and elongated oval. The entire road is bisected through the middle by the 8½ mile long Plantation Trail (TR 101) that follows an east to west orientation. Most of the trails in the Canaan Mountain Area cross or connect with this trail. There is an 8-person shelter near the junction of the Davis Trail and Plantation Trail for use as over-night camping.

The best place to access the trail system on Canaan Mountain is to enter CLR from Route 32 near Canaan Heights. The first 10 miles of this road have been covered with a good base of crushed stone, making the road easy to drive in any type of vehicle. This section of the road follows a portion of Red Run for several miles.

The road begins to get a little rough at the western end, just beyond the western terminus of Plantation Trail, where it turns north back towards Blackwater Falls State Park. Just outside of Blackwater Falls State Park the road is passable with four-wheel drive vehicles only. Unless you have a vehicle capable of crossing rugged stream beds and up a slippery rock wall, **do not continue on CLR from Blackwater Falls State Park**.

Allegheny Trail

The Canaan/Blackwater Cross Country Ski Trail discussed under the Davis Trail above, also serves as a section of the Allegheny Trail. In the early 1970's a group of volunteers formed an organization, the *West Virginia Scenic Trails Association,* to create a 300-mile trail from north to south through West Virginia. The trail begins at the Mason Dixon Line on the West Virginia/Pennsylvania border and ends in Monroe County, West Virginia.

Where possible, the Allegheny Trail follows existing trails and roads throughout its length, but several new trails were made in between the existing ones to create an uninterrupted trail system. The Allegheny Trail is well marked with yellow blazes on trees and rocks throughout its length. With the support of several natural resource agencies at the state and federal level, volunteers keep the trail in good shape. The Allegheny Trail meanders through Blackwater Falls State Park providing a link between the trails on Canaan Mountain with those on Backbone Mountain. **However, the trail is interrupted near the park boundary by strip mines.** For more information about the Allegheny Trail write to: West Virginia Scenic Trails Association, PO Box 4042, Charleston, WV 2536; or for maps, write to WVSTA Publications, 633 West Virginia Avenue, Morgantown, WV, 26505.

Tablerock Overlook Trail

The view from the end of this leisurely, one mile meander through an open hardwoods forest is one of the most engrossing vistas in the area. To access the trail you will need to drive nearly the full length of the fairly level, well-graveled section of CLR (approx. 9 ½ miles from Route 32). The trailhead is marked and there is a small parking area available at the trailhead.

The trail is blazed with blue markings that are somewhat faded and widely spaced. However, the trail is well worn from heavy use and is easy to follow. The trail will take you on a gentle climb through an open hardwoods forest to a high point. From there, it will descend somewhat through a rocky, boggy section where rhododendron colonies become the predominant vegetation. Soon, the trail exits the rhododendron onto a large rock outcrop high above Red Run. The broad, "rock table" extends in an arc to the right where you can peer down into the canyon from various vantage points.

From the overlook, the view extends over several mountains all the way to Shaver's Mountain. Near the overlook, there is a nice campsite. It is available on a first-come, first-serve basis. This trail and the view it affords are well worth a leisurely morning. Bring your lunch and plan on staying a while. The expansive vista and wide-open skies will hold you captive for as long as the weather and time permits.

*For a complete list of trails in the Canaan Mountain Area contact the Cheat Ranger District of the Monongahela National Forest at PO Box 368, Parsons, WV 26287 or call 304/478-325. Also, the Highlands Conservancy has published a book describing the trails in the Mon, titled *Monongahela National Forest Hiking Guide*, by Allen de Hart and Bruce Sundqueist.

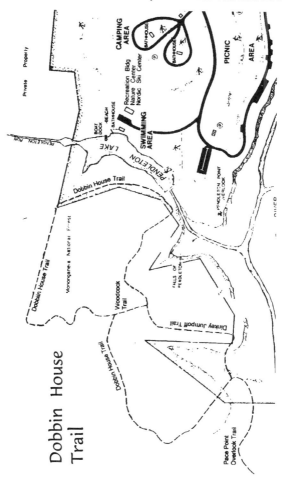

Dobbin House Trail

Canaan Valley State Park

Located in Canaan Valley, ten miles south of Blackwater Falls State Park off Rt. 32. Call 1-800/callwva Monday - Friday 8:00 AM - 5:00 PM for details.

Located in one West Virginia's most unique geological and biological reserves, Canaan Valley State Park offers something for everyone. The park abounds in rare plant and animal communities for those who love nature. A diverse network of trails affords access to interesting plant communities and ample opportunities for the hiker year-round.

Winter is a wonderful time to visit the park if you like down-hill or cross-country skiing, ice skating and snow-shoe trekking. The elevation of the park ranges from 3200 feet to 4,400 feet at the top of the ski slope. The average annual snow fall is about 120 inches per year.

Snow making machines were built at the down-hill facility to ensure good snow cover during the milder winters experienced since the 1970's. There are two chair lifts on the ski slopes, trails for every level of skier, and instructors are available.

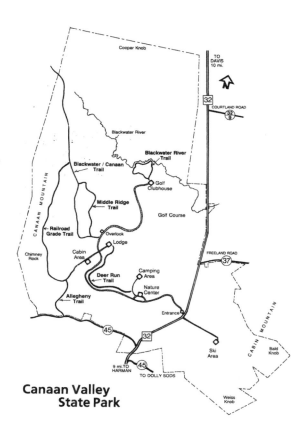

Canaan Valley State Park

Cathedral State Park

Located on US Route 50 near Aurora, West Virginia. Contact Park Superintendent at Blackwater Falls State park for more information at 304/259-5216, or 1-800/callwva, Monday - Friday 8:00 AM - 5:00 PM.

Cathedral State Park is a 133 acre mixed forest of virgin hemlock and northern hardwoods species. Step just a few yards down one of its trails under the towering canopy, and you will experience the illusion of a changeless, timeless world. The forest here is a tiny glimmer of the primeval forests which flourished for thousands of years before human footsteps broke ground on this continent.

Trees in this rare stand of virgin timber were living before Columbus crossed the Atlantic. Myriad shades of green block much of the sunlight from the forest floor. Tiny windows created by the interlocking branches 60 to 120 feet above, allow a few golden rays to pierce the dark depths of this complex plant community.

Thick, rich-carpets of various species of moss cover the ground, extend up standing tree trunks and over the carcasses of those fallen giants heaped in all directions, in this true "old growth forest." Many species of lichens and fungi thrive in the damp, somber recesses in a network of trails cross the sparkling waters of a stream, through sprawling rhododendron thickets and around scaly buttresses of the huge trees.

Lush stands of ferns and a few wildflowers line the trails and meandering stream. Painted trillium, Canada mayflower, partridge berry are just a few of the spring flowers you might find. Tall wands of cinnamon fern wave gently in tandem with the heavy limbs of the hemlocks in the slightest breeze.

On the most sultry summer day, you may find a natural retreat in the cool shade of Cathedral State Park. The park is located at a relatively high elevation of 2,600 feet, adding to the slightly milder summer temperatures. However, the winters are severe here. The sagging, broken limbs seen on many of the trees are the victims of heavy snows and occasional ice storms which may turn the forest into a giant ice sculpture for days.

Hiking and cross-country skiing are possible across the several miles of trails weaving through the park. Picnic tables and a picnic shelter are available for day use, year-round. Everyone should see Cathedral State Park, not just to experience its beauty and serenity, but to know what we lost when the wilderness was crushed to make room for our civilization.

Dolly Sods Wilderness and Scenic Areas

This expanse of wilderness atop the Allegheny plateau may be accessed from State Route 32, south of Canaan Valley by way of Laneville Road. From Canaan Valley, make a left turn onto Laneville Road and follow this twisting, narrow road for about 7 miles until you cross a large wooden bridge over Red Creek. Once you have crossed the bridge, you are in Laneville. Across from the DNR cabin, turn right onto a gravel road for a long ascent to the top of Dolly Sods. Check with the Monongahela National Forest for more information on trails, camping and maps to this wilderness area; Monongahela National Forest 304/636-1800.

There is no easy way to reach the incredible scenery, unusual plant-life, expansive bogs and beaver dams located on this wonderful mountaintop plateau. From either of three access points, you have a long, steep, windy drive up a narrow gravel road. But the opportunities for hiking, wildlife viewing, botanizing and scenic wonders make the trip well worth it.

A very exciting annual event held in the Dolly Sods Scenic area is the migratory bird

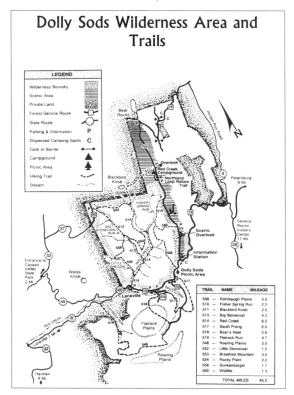

Dolly Sods Wilderness Area and Trails

LEGEND

Wilderness Boundary	
Scenic Area	
Private Land	
Forest Service Route	
State Route	
Parking & Information	P
Dispersed Camping Spots	C
Gate or Barrier	
Campground	▲
Picnic Area	
Hiking Trail	
Stream	

TRAIL	NAME	MILEAGE
508	Rohrbaugh Plains	3.5
510	Fisher Spring Run	2.3
511	Blackbird Knob	2.5
513	Big Stonecoal	4.3
514	Red Creek	6.2
517	South Prong	2.6
518	Boar's Nest	2.6
519	Flatrock Run	4.7
548	Roaring Plains	3.0
552	Little Stonecoal	1.5
553	Breathed Mountain	3.5
554	Rocky Point	2.2
558	Dunkenbarger	1.6
560	Wildlife	1.3
	TOTAL MILES	**45.3**

banding and bird count, held during September. The Allegheny Front Migratory Observatory Station, operated by the Brooks Bird Club is across the road from Red Creek Campground. The operation begun by the Brooks Bird Club is actually a cooperative effort between the Monongahela National Forest and the West Virginia Division of Natural Resources.

In the effort to study the population dynamics of migratory birds, the station bands nearly 6000 birds in some years. The work is done by volunteers who camp on the mountain in order to be ready to open the nets just before dawn, when the birds begin moving. The banding station welcomes visitors, and believes in educating the public about the importance of the work and the importance of birds in the ecosystem. Contact the Naturalists at Blackwater Falls and Canaan Valley State Parks for more information about Dolly Sods and the banding station.

Fairfax Stone Historic Monument

This four-acre historical park may be reached by following 219 north from Thomas about four miles. A sign on the right side of the road will direct you to turn right and follow a gravel road for two miles to the parking lot beside the marker.

For a discussion of the historical events leading up to the establishment of the "Fairfax Stone," refer to the first pages of the chapter titled *Human History*. One of the oldest monuments in the United States,the original stone placed at the site in 1746 was destroyed by vandalism in the 1850's. It was replaced three times; with the last one having been placed in 1957 by the West Virginia Conservation Commission.

The stone marks the spot dividing the original land grant of Lord Baltimore (Maryland and parts of Pennsylvania) and the six million acre land grant deeded to the Fairfax family.

The Fairfax Stone currently lies near the boundary between West Virginia and Maryland and marks the corners of Grant, Preston and Tucker Counties in West Virginia. A survey line was made in 1746 from the head waters of the Rappahannock located in Shenandoah National Forest, to the headwaters of the North Branch of the Potomac where the stone is placed.

The survey line marked the boundary between Maryland and what was then Virginia. The boundary was challenged by the State of Maryland in the Federal Court System and the challenge was defeated each time.

The monument site is a quiet, tree-lined open field with a tiny spring in the center. The marking of this tiny spring as the headwaters of the Potomac River had a major impact on the history of Virginia, West Virginia and Maryland.

215

CALENDAR OF EVENTS:
THINGS TO DO AT
BLACKWATER FALLS STATE PARK

<u>December—March</u>
Cross-country skiing (equipment rentals available)
Snowshoe walking (equipment rentals available)
Hiking/Guided Walks
Sledding

<u>May</u>
Family Trails Day Hike (guided hike along Blackwater/Canaan Ski Trail, 8 miles)
Wildflower Pilgrimage (guided wildflower walks throughout Tucker County)
Century Day Bird Count

<u>June—August</u>
Non-Game Wildlife Weekend (weekend long series of workshops and hikes about mammals, reptiles, birds, butterflies and insects, fun for all ages)

For more information about
events and facilities at the park
just call
1-800-CALLWV.

Bike Rentals
Guided Walks and other nature programs

<u>September</u>
September Senior Fling
Astronomy Weekend

<u>October</u>
Wild Walks Weekend (hike between the
parks as above in May)
Astronomy Weekend

REFERENCES

Brooks, A.B. 1911. *Forestry and Wood Industries.* West Virginia Geological Survey, Vol. 5. Acme Publishing Company, Morgantown, West Virginia.

Clarkson, R.B. 1964. *Tumult on The Mountains: Lumbering in West Virginia, 1770 - 1920.* McClain Printing Company, Parsons, WV.

Davis, Rebecca Harding 1880. *By-Paths in the Mountains.* Harpers New Monthly Magazine.

Core, E.L. 1966. *The Vegetation of West Virginia.* McClain Printing Company, Parsons, WV.

Fansler, H.F. 1962. *History of Tucker County, West Virginia.* McClain Printing Company, Parsons,WV.

Kennedy, P.P. 1853. *The Blackwater Chronicle, A narrative of an Expedition Into the Land of Canaan in Randolph County, VA.* Redfield New York.

Ludlum, John C. 1964. *Blackwater Falls State Park. Resources, geology and recreation.* The West Virginia Geological and Economic Survey.

Mott, *History of Davis and Canaan Valley.*

Robinson, F. G. 1953. *Davis, West Virginia, Village of Undying Hope.* Tableland Trails 1:25-47.

Strausbaugh, P.D. and Core, E.L. *Flora of West Virginia.*

Thompson, G.B. 1974. *History of Logging in Davis, West Virginia, 1884-1924.* McClain Printing Company, Parsons, West Virginia.

Wayland, J.W. 1925. *The Fairfax Line: Thomas Lewis's Journal of 1746.* Henkel Press, New Market, Virginia.

Regional Historical Map

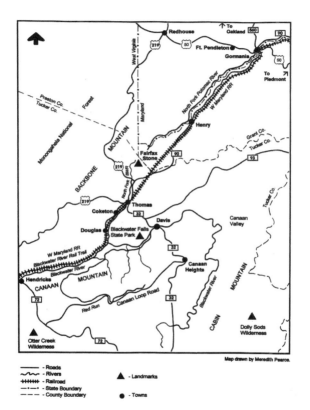

Map drawn by Meredith Pearce.

——— - Roads	▲ - Landmarks
∿∿ - Rivers	
+++++ - Railroad	● - Towns
—·—·— - State Boundary	
— — — - County Boundary	

Index